Kermit Schafer Presents
BLOOPER TUBE
BASED ON RADIO-TV'S MOST HILARIOUS AWARD-WINNING BLOOPERS!

A Special Collection
The Best of 25 years of TV Bloopers
Including the History of Bloopers

Crown Publishers, Inc.
New York

Manufactured in the United States of America

Library of Congress Cataloging in Publication Data

Schafer, Kermit, 1914-
    Kermit Schafer presents Blooper tube

    Includes index.
    1. Television broadcasting—United States—
Anecdotes, facetiae, satire, etc. I. Title.
II. Title: Blooper tube.
PN1992.58.S3   791.45'02907   78-31706
ISBN 0-517-53789-3
ISBN 0-517-53709-7 pbk.

Second Printing, July, 1979

BLOOPER MAN

Lyrics from Theme Music of BLUNDERFUL WORLD OF BLOOPERS TV Special

Music by Laurie Hannan

There once was a guy named Freud,
Whose slips of the lips he couldn't avoid,
They brought him world fame.
Then there was Reverend Spooner,
Whose mixed up words he spoke abnormally sooner,
And proved a trip of the lip is no shame.
Then along came Schafer,
Whom we shout hip, hip, hooray for,
Blooper Man is his name,
Bloopers are the name of his game.

Bloop, Bloop, Bloop, Everybody Bloops, and it can even happen to you.
Bloop, Bloop, Everybody Bloops, and when you do, it's hard to undo.
If you happen to Bloop when Mr. Blooper's around,
He'll share the fun with everyone in town,
'Cause if you make a fluff, he's gonna love your stuff,
He'll pick you up when you've fallen down.

He's the Super Duper Blooper Man,
Bringing joy and laughter whenever he can.
Preserves the Bloopers like vintage wine,
Says to forgive is human, to err is divine.

So when some of your words come out wrong,
Or they're where they shouldn't belong,
You've said it, now forget it,
Join in the Blooper Song.

On Radio and TV,
Or just little old you and me,
Bloopers will always be.

. . . This conclees . . . this concloos . . . that is all.

Kermit Schafer
Blooper Man

DEDICATION

I wish to thank the various members of the entertainment industry pictured in the photo-biography portion of this documentary for the part they played in my career.

I also wish to thank the members of the broadcasting industry for their cooperation in making BLOOPER TUBE possible.

The Video Blooper portion of BLOOPER TUBE is a catalogue of unintended indiscretions before microphone and camera covering a 25-year span from the early pioneer days of television, in which I was fortunate to play a part, to present-day TV. It contains all types of Bloopers, known in broadcasting by various names, such as Fluffs, Goofs, Slips, Flubs, Bleeps, etc.

The material in this collection is authentic and was gathered from video tapes, kinescopes, sound tracks, off-the-air recordings, and other bona fide sources. Some of the Video Blooper photos were changed to help portray the actuality of the incident depicted.

Alexander Pope said, "To err is human, to forgive divine." He must have had in mind those who have spent anguished and painful moments reliving some of these incidents ... It is to the victim of the Blooper that this sympathetic tribute is dedicated.

CONTENTS

BLOOPER TUBE

A VERITABLE HISTORY OF BROADCASTING
INCLUDING RARE AND EXCLUSIVE PHOTOGRAPHS

Research:
Meredith Conover

A special thanks to Blooper Researcher Meredith Conover who also is my valuable assistant. It would be difficult enough putting this Blooper documentary together if the material were normal and straight. However, her sanity and enthusiasm for BLOOPER TUBE never waivered.

Kermit Schafer

Portions of the video stills are from BLOOPER TUBE, feature-length movie, formerly titled PARDON MY BLOOPER and distributed by K-Tel International.

All material herein copyright by Blooper Enterprises, Inc. / a div. of Kermit Schafer Productions, Suite 840, 1320 South Dixie Highway, Coral Gables, Florida 33146

INTRODUCTION

JOHNNY CARSON in his introduction of Kermit Schafer as a guest on his NBC-TV TONIGHT SHOW, celebrating the 10th Anniversary of Bloopers on which Carson was given 10 Blooper albums, said:

Producer Kermit Schafer has been active in Radio and Television for quite a few years, and for some time he has made a speciality of collecting what are known as fluffs or goofs . . . or blowing up in your lines, commonly known as Bloopers. These are the things unplanned on television shows . . . radio programs . . . the things announcers and actors say. He's compiled Bloopers that have happened throughout the country. They read just about as funny as when they occurred on the air . . . He's also made albums.

Bloopers fascinate most people in and out of the business too . . . These are great.

10th
YEAR OF
BLOOPERS

FOREWORD

MIKE DOUGLAS in the Foreword to Kermit Schafer's BLUNDERFUL WORLD OF BLOOPERS book, celebrating the 25th Silver Anniversary of Bloopers, wrote:

When Kermit Schafer appeared on my show, I cried. I cried with joy over the funniest segment we ever did—Kermit's presentation of Bloopers.

What impressed me most about Kermit's long-time endeavor to gather broadcasting's funniest mistakes was the fact that no one is immune to these lip slippers. When they happen, there's nothing to do but accept them. There's no cure for Blooperitis. There is a partial remedy—tape.

While tape has been great for programming, it does, honestly, take some of the spontaneity out of entertainment; with the unused portions of a show also goes the Blooper—on to the editing room floor.

Thankfully, though, Kermit Schafer came along 25 years ago to preserve the goofs of our generation for prosperity—oops! I mean posterity.

To Kermit Schafer, thanks for helping us all learn to laugh at ourselves.

25th
YEAR OF
BLOOPERS

PART 1: THE BLOOPER TUBE

I have often been asked if Blooper victims resent my collecting their boners and making them public. The contrary is true. I like to believe that it is the result of their confidence in me over the years for the good taste that I have always striven for in the preservation of their miscues. I respect and value their trust, and I, therefore, exercise great care so as not to single out anyone to embarrass. I believe that the following words aptly express the attitude of the majority of Blooper victims.

"I am never more tickled than when I laugh at myself."
                                        MARK TWAIN

In the presentation of all of my Blooper works, my primary aim is humor. Bloopers are meant to be funny, not vulgar. As for the profanity often associated with Bloopers, it does not offend anyone who can keep an open mind about the reality of human error in broadcasting. The public is quick to enjoy and to forgive when performers under great strain slip on the verbal banana peel.

"There are certain trying moments in which profanity furnishes a relief denied even to prayer."

MARK TWAIN

12

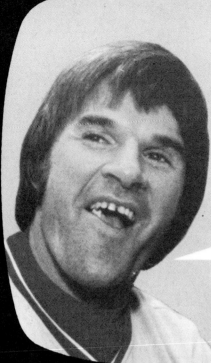

17

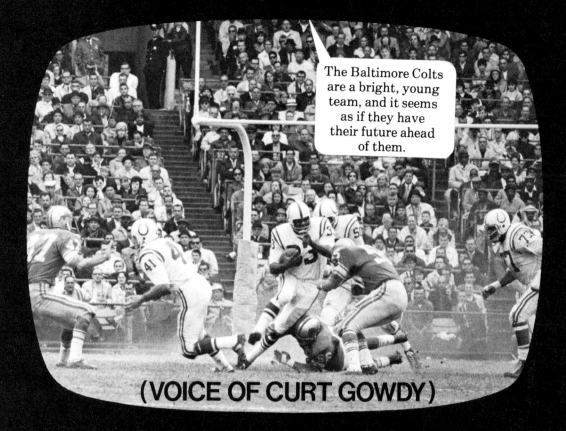

Stay queened for "Tune for a Day" . . .
QUEEN FOR A DAY

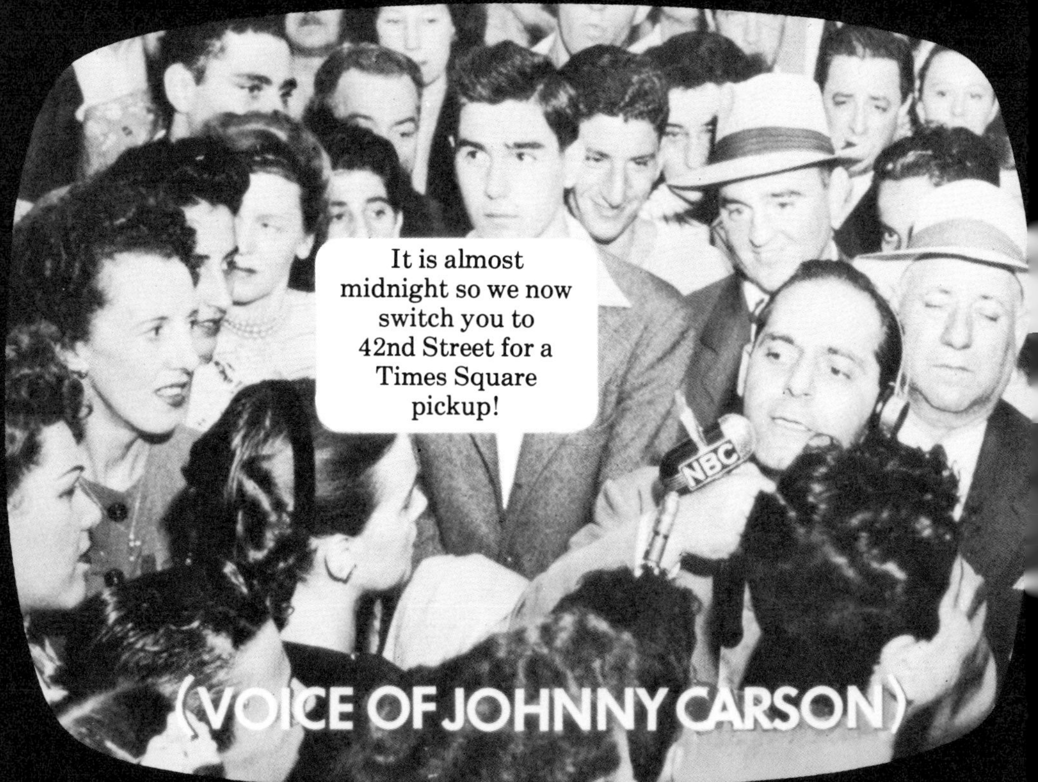
It is almost midnight so we now switch you to 42nd Street for a Times Square pickup!
NBC
(VOICE OF JOHNNY CARSON)

20

APOLLO:
FIRST MANNED FLIGHT

Stay tuned for the Apollo Looney landings on the moon!

Juan Pizzaro is on the verge of pissing a no-hitter!

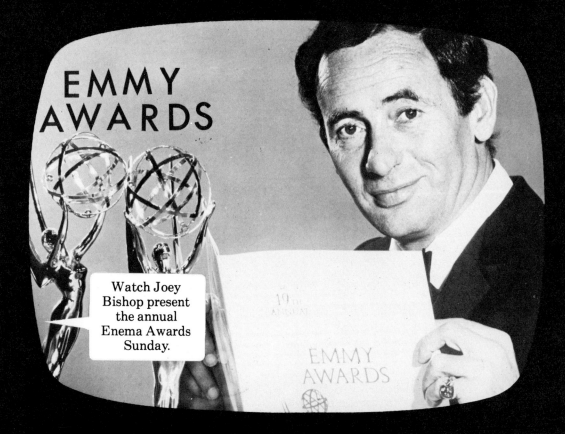

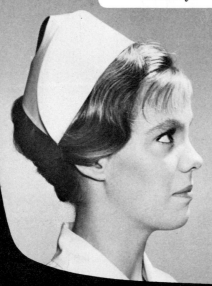

Senator Margaret Chase Smith
How would you react if you woke up in the White House one morning?
I would apologize to Mrs. Eisenhower and go home immediately.

(VOICE OF BUFFALO BOB)
HOWDY DOODY
PEANUT GALLERY
Kenneth, did you do anything wrong?
I farted.

28

Stay tuned for "I Love Loosely."
i love

In the Mid East . . . Lesbian forces attacked Israel . . . Lesbanese . . . LEBANESE!!
CYPRUS
Limassol
Larnaca
Famagusta
Tarabulus
(Tripoli)
Homs
Tadmor
Beirut
SEA
Damascus
(Dimishq)
En Nebk
Haifa
Sea of Galilee
Tel Aviv-
Jaffa
ISRAEL
Amman
Jerusalem
Hebron
Port Said
Gaza
El Mansura
El Qantara
Ismailia
Suez Canal
El Karak
JORDAN
CAIRO
Suez
Sinai
Ma'an

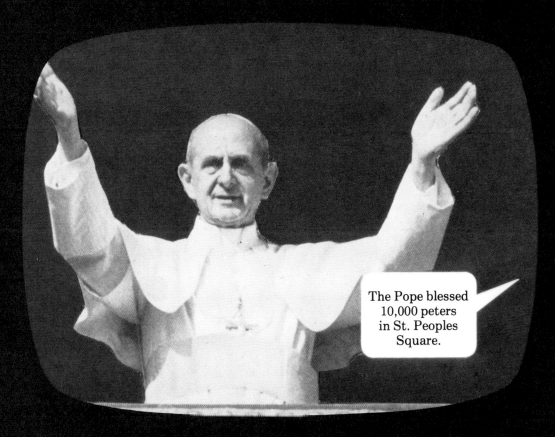

I'm a maid for a large family of four boys, three girls, one adult and one adultress.

A Tale Of Two Cities"
Tonight's Late Show features Dickens' immortal "Sale of Two Titties."

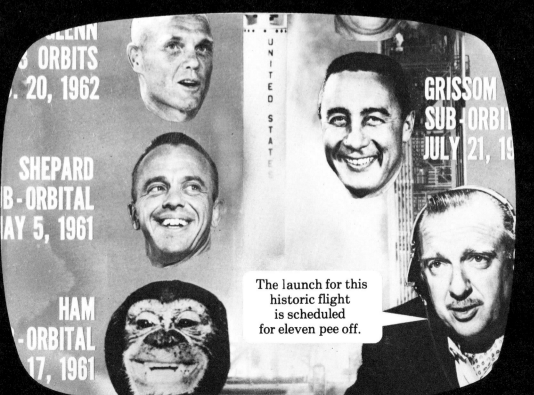

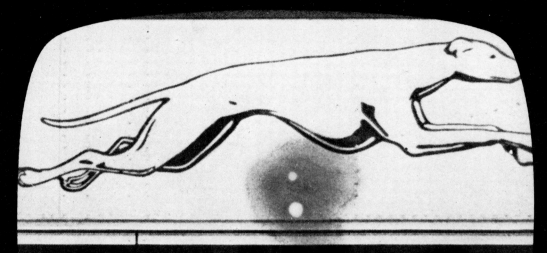

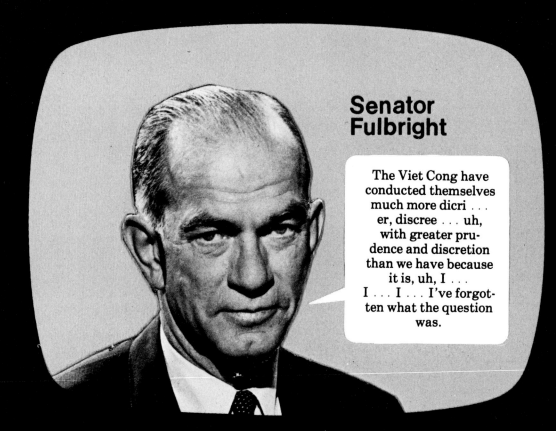

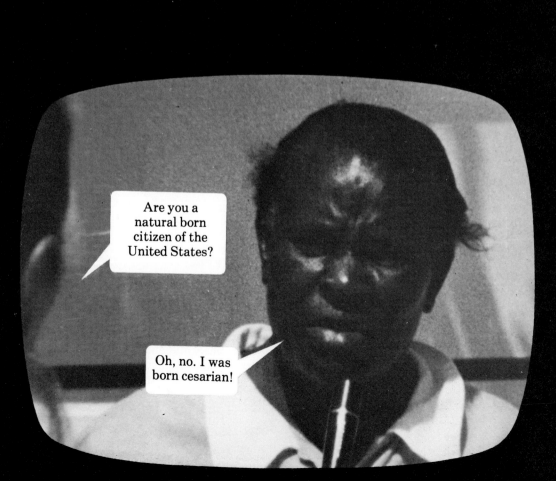

THE NEW LORETTA YOUNG SHOW

See a brand-new repeat of the old "New Loretta Young Show."

In yesterday's round she took a douche on the hole . . . DUCE!!

CBS BOWLING CLASSIC

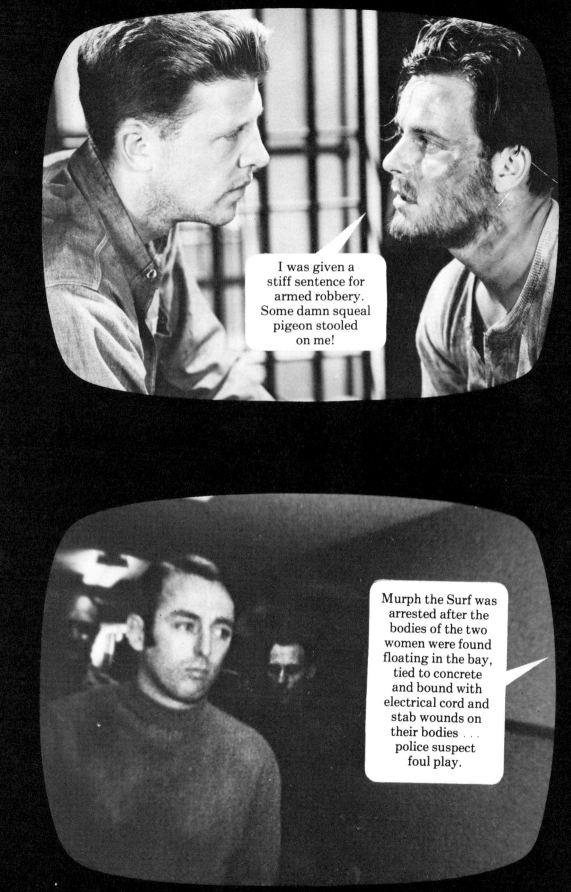

60

How many children do you have, and what does your husband do for a living?
I have 13 children . . . my husband operates an automatic screwing machine.

He's so sexy. Whenever I see him, my heart goes peter, peter.
CHARO

CIMARRON CITY
SHERIFF'S
OFFIC
See the adventures of the Cimarron Shitty Sheriff on NBC.

WEATHER BULLETIN!
Here is a weather bulletin! The Mayor has just ordered residents adjacent to the Mill River to ejaculate immediately!!

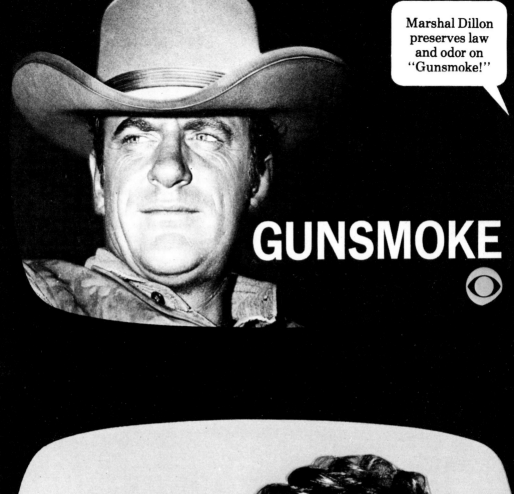

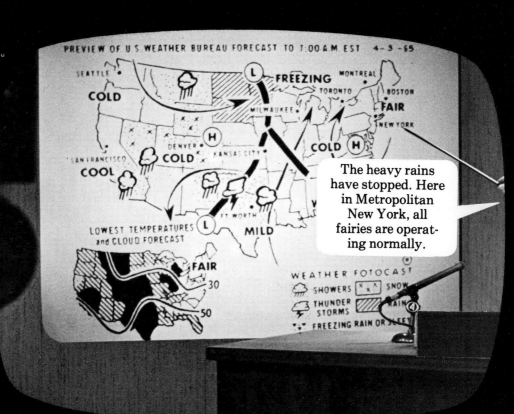

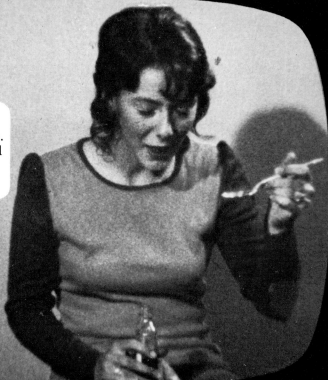

84

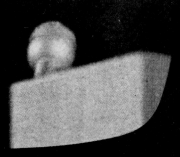

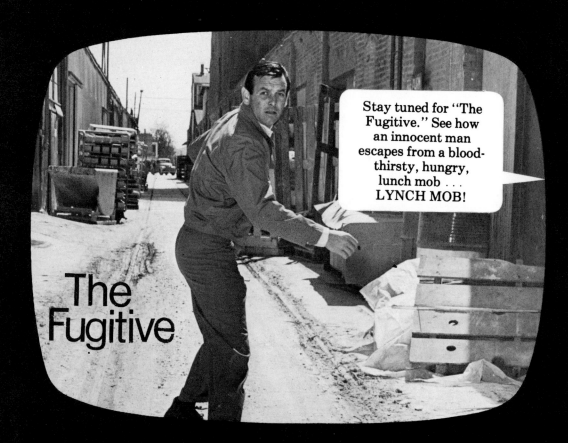

The Soviets sent up a rocket to test the effect of space on man's orgasm . . . I mean, organism!

Now, kids, a Walt Disney medley, "Hi Diddley Dee," "When You Wish Upon A Star," and "I've Seen Everything When I've Seen An Elephant's Fly." ELEPHANT FLY!!

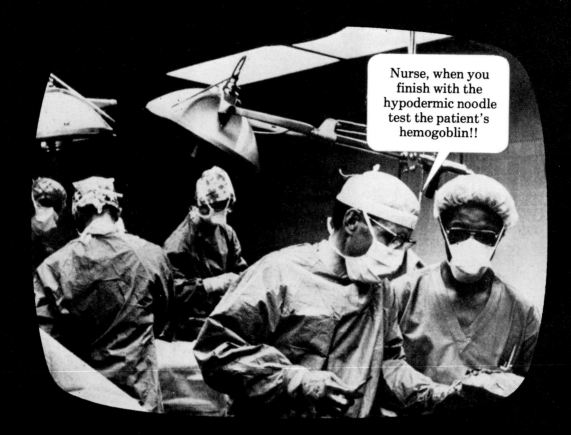

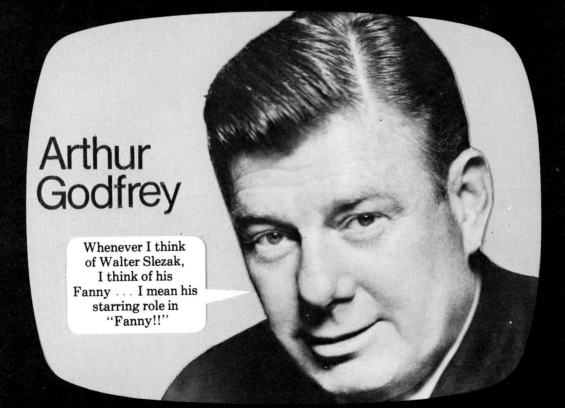

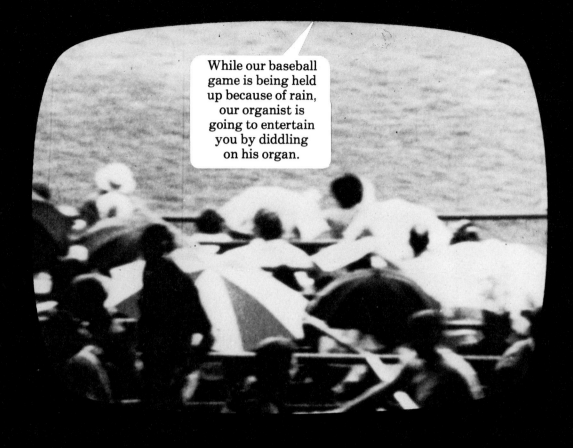

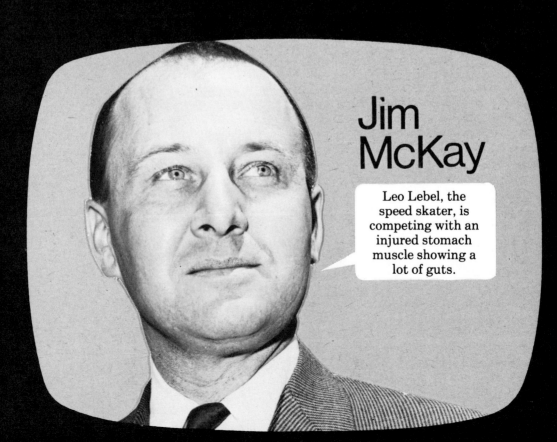

That's the weather from Anchorage. Now I'll take a leak out the window to see if it's freezing outside our studio.

Police found the body of a half nude man stuffed into a sewer pipe. The death was called sewerside.

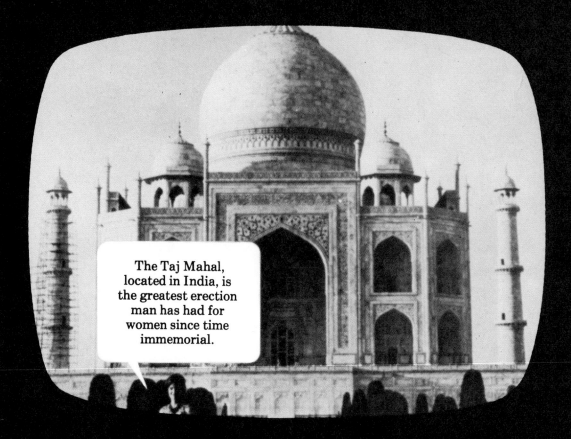

106

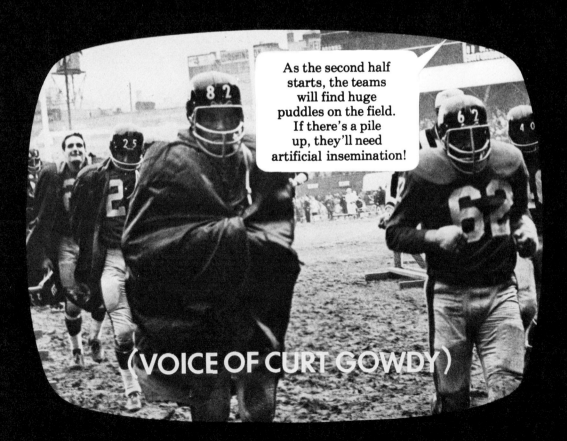

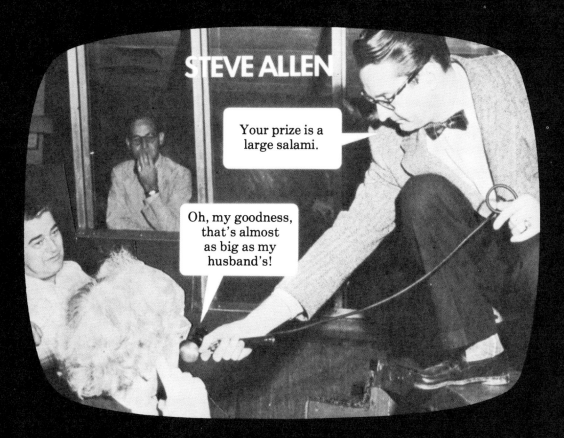

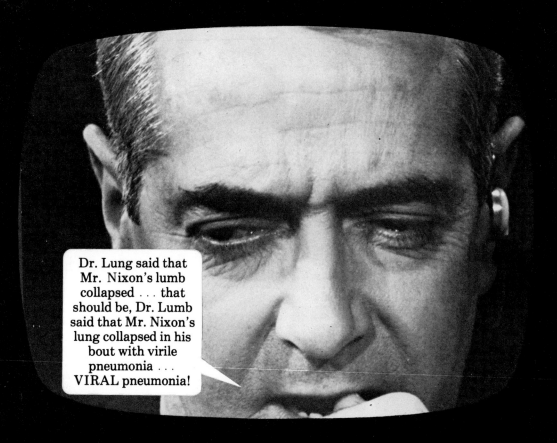

PART 2: IN THE BEGINNING

EDITOR'S NOTE

The huge flow of mail from Blooper fans from all over the world and from all walks of life reached several millions long ago. Most of the letter writers wanted to know more about Kermit Schafer and the origins of the Blooper phenomenon that provided so much enjoyment. Here is the story from the beginning.

**ABOUT
KERMIT SCHAFER**
BOY PRODUCER

I was born in the Borough Park section of Brooklyn. In the proximity of a few blocks lived some assorted and distinguished neighbors. On the same street was Norman Cousins who grew up to be the Editor of the SATURDAY REVIEW OF LITERATURE in addition to other distinguished accomplishments. Bennett Cerf sent both Norman and me a photo he discovered, together with a letter in which he said, "I am sending you this photo of the graduating class of P.S. 103 with the countenance of yourself, boy producer, and that of Norman Cousins, boy editor." Another luminary on the block was Herbert Aptheker, a resident of dubious fame, who was a member of the same public school graduating class and who went on to become America's number one member of the Communist party. A couple of good song writers also were neighbors. Max Gittler, who worked in a grocery store, became Mac Gordon of the song writing team of Gordon and Revel which wrote many hits. Also a neighbor was Sam Coslow who wrote "Cocktails for Two," several Bing Crosby hits, the Dean Martin theme song, "Everybody Loves Somebody Sometime," and the PARDON MY BLOOPER movie theme song, "You Blew It!" A few blocks away lived Allen Funt of CANDID CAMERA fame; also Henry Jaffee who was the attorney for the greats, such as Frank Sinatra and Dinah Shore, and with whom I have had dealings over the years. He is the producer and owner of the DINAH TV package in addition to producing other major TV Specials.

Norman Cousins   Schafer   Herbert Aptheker

KERMIT SCHAFER   1914–1979

RADIO / TV / FILM / RECORDING PRODUCER

and
Director ● Writer ● Film Editor ● Audio Tape Editor
Video Tape Editor ● Sound Man ● Engineer ● Record Manufacturer
Performer ● Commercial Copywriter ● Publicist ● Artist
Layout Man ● Movie Camera Man ● Projectionist ● Lecturer
Photographer ● Advertising Director ● Creative Director
Salesman ● Talent Agent ● Lyricist ● Promoter ● Author

And other odd jobs

EARLY-DAY RADIO

Kermit Schafer started his career in broadcasting as a teenager doubling as a page boy and a radio producer. While he was going to high school, he maintained a theatrical office in the RKO Building in Radio City, New York. His various endeavors included his handling of the exclusive radio rights to the Olympic Games in Berlin, Germany, in 1936. His long service and achievements qualify him as a pioneer in the broadcasting field. He is a member of the Radio Pioneers Club which is comprised of veterans of the broadcast industry who have served 25 years in radio.

PAGE BOY

RADIO GREATS left to right: Veteran announcer Don Wilson of Jack Benny fame; Arch Obler, creator of LIGHTS OUT; Kenny Delmar, also known as "Senator Claghorn"; Mike Douglas; singer Patti Paige; and Schafer, celebrating the 25th Anniversary of **Bloopers** on the Mike Douglas Show.

Veteran broadcasting great Lowell Thomas shown with Schafer who was his guest at Thomas' estate in Pawling, Dutchess County, New York. Schafer originated his COLONEL STOOPNAGLE radio show from Thomas' broadcasting studio, which was converted from a barn. It was here that he first learned of Thomas' great sense of humor that resulted in his memorable breakups which are immortalized in Schafer's Blooper works.

Lowell Thomas' radio broadcasting studio.

Colonel Lemuel Q. Stoopnagle, one of radio's best-known comedians who was part of the original team of Stoopnagle and Budd.

Met opera star Lauritz Melchior, Metropolitan Opera Treasurer Earl Lewis, Ted Cott, program emcee, appearing on RCA Victor's radio program co-produced by Schafer. Melchior is relating the classic Blooper that occurred in a live broadcast of LOHENGRIN from the Met. A swan which was supposed to carry him off stage left early. An amused radio audience overheard him ask in his Nordic accent, "Can anyone tell me vot time does the next svan leave?"

Actor-comedian Keenan Wynn who appeared regularly on the COLONEL STOOPNAGLE Show.

RADIO SOAP OPERA

I had the good fortune to be part of the Golden Age of Radio as well as Television. As the saying goes, I paid my dues in both media. Although starting as a youngster in radio, I served in many capacities in the production of Soap Operas including that of a casting director and producer. One of the "Soaps" that I produced, in association with Roger White in New York, was SOCIETY GIRL which was a daytime "strip" program on the CBS Radio network, broadcast in 1940.

SOCIETY GIRL was based on the New York socialite and debutante, Brenda Frazier, and her sophisticated travels around New York City in such posh places as the Stork Club and 21.

SOCIETY GIRL, like many Soap operas of that period, such as DAVID HARUM, OUR GAL SUNDAY, etc., was presented "live," which was another way of saying that I had fits five days a week due to the strain of never being quite sure of what disasters were going to plague our program during the fifteen minutes of time which the red second hand on the clock told us, in no uncertain terms, was all we had each weekday. I was not alone in this constant trepidation. "Fluffs," as they were known in those days, occurred on all radio shows, such as the one where the sound effects man ran into difficulty when sound effects were done live, unlike recordings which are used today.

ACTOR: Okay, you rat, I'm going to drill ya . . . take that!! (CLICK OF GUN—NO SHOTS) Okay, you rat . . . now I'm really going to drill you!! (CLICK OF GUN—NO SHOTS) On second thought . . . I'm gonna take this knife and slit your throat!! (TWO SHOTS FIRED)

ANNOUNCER: Tune in tomorrow to learn if John will goose Sadie's cook . . . I mean, cook Sadie's goose!!

Left to right: Charlotte Manson, who had the lead role in SOCIETY GIRL; Producer Schafer; and Brenda Joyce, Hollywood movie actress who starred in the Hollywood version of SOCIETY GIRL.

A RADIO BLOOPER NIGHTMARE WAR OF THE WORLDS

Nothing in the annals of broadcasting made a greater impact on America than the Orson Welles WAR OF THE WORLDS dramatization based on the H. G. Wells classic. I had the privilege to write and produce a capsulized version of this historic radio event in my PARDON MY BLOOPER feature-length motion picture. The following is transcribed, in part, from the Howard Koch written CBS memorable presentation which has been immortalized in schools throughout the nation as a part of American history.

DOCUMENTARY ANNOUNCER: October, 1938 ... While America slumbered in a period of calm after World War I, a war to end all wars, in Europe Adolph Hitler's alliance was making plans for the conquest of the Free World which he hoped to crush under the heels of his new form of tyranny, Nazism. In America October 30, 1938, was Halloween night. Millions of American families were safe in their homes enjoying the entertainment of their favorite radio programs in an era of peace ... In New York City a group of professional actors in the Mercury Theatre, under the direction of Orson Welles, were about to present the famous H. G. Wells' story WAR OF THE WORLDS, a radio program that would startle most of the nation and which turned out to be a Blooper nightmare for the broadcast industry. The next voice that you will hear will be that of the distinguished American actor, Orson Welles, in the role of Dr. Pearson, Scientist.

WELLES: Of the creatures in the rocket cylinder at Grover Mills, I can give you no authoritative information either to their nature, their origin, nor their purpose here on earth. For want of a better word, I shall refer to the mysterious weapons as a heat ray.

ACTOR: Thank you, Professor Pearson. Ladies and gentlemen, I have a grave announcement to make. Incredible as it may seem, both the observation of science and the evidence of our eyes lead to the inescapable assumption that those strange beings that landed in the Jersey farmland tonight are the vanguard of an invading army from the planet Mars!!

Actor, Writer, Producer, Director Orson Welles.

A harried and apologetic Orson Welles telling the press that it was all a hoax.

Right: Radio actor Kenny Delmar who, as a member of Orson Welles's Mercury Theatre, played a major role in the WAR OF THE WORLDS Halloween hoax. He is relating to Mike Douglas and Schafer about his portrayal of President Franklin D. Roosevelt's telling the nation that Doomsday had arrived so realistically that it was believed by countless terrified listeners.

THE NEW YORK TIMES, OCTOBER 31, 1938.

Radio Listeners in Panic, Taking War Drama as Fact

Many Flee Homes to Escape 'Gas Raid From Mars'—Phone Calls Swamp Police at Broadcast of Wells Fantasy

A wave of mass hysteria seized thousands of radio listeners throughout the nation between 8:15 and 9:30 o'clock last night when a broadcast of a dramatization of H. G. Wells's fantasy, "The War of the Worlds," led thousands to believe that an interplanetary conflict had started with invading Martians spreading wide death and destruction in New Jersey and New York.

The broadcast, which disrupted households, interrupted religious services, created traffic jams and clogged communications systems, was made by Orson Welles, who as the radio character, "The Shadow," used to give "the creeps" to countless child listeners. This time at least a score of adults required medical treatment for shock and hysteria.

In Newark, in a single block at Heddon Terrace and Hawthorne Avenue, more than twenty families rushed out of their houses with wet handkerchiefs and towels over their faces to flee from what they believed was to be a gas raid. Some began moving household furniture.

Throughout New York families left their homes, some to flee to near-by parks. Thousands of persons called the police, newspapers and radio stations here and in other cities of the United States and Canada seeking advice on protective measures against the raids.

The program was produced by Mr. Welles and the Mercury Theatre on the Air over station WABC and the Columbia Broadcasting System's coast-to-coast network, from 8 to 9 o'clock.

The radio play, as presented, was to simulate a regular radio program with a "break-in" for the material of the play. The radio listeners, apparently, missed or did not listen to the introduction, which was: "The Columbia Broadcasting System and its affiliated stations present Orson Welles and the Mercury Theatre on the Air in 'The War of the Worlds' by H. G. Wells."

They also failed to associate the program with the newspaper listing of the program, announced as "Today: 8:00-9:00—Play: H. G. Wells's 'War of the Worlds'—WABC." They ignored three additional announcements made during the broadcast emphasizing its fictional nature

Mr. Welles opened the program with a description of the series of

Continued on Page Four

RADIO NEW YORK/HOLLYWOOD

My radio career expanded from New York to Hollywood. Shown are some of the people with whom I worked, which indicates that Bloopers were not an overnight success, but rather the result of many long years of experience in the entertainment industry, including that of a talent agent. I endeavored to sell Bernard Zanville to Hollywood before his name change to Dane Clark. I had cast him in a role in SOCIETY GIRL, a CBS soap opera on radio. Zanville was a New Utrecht High School graduate in Brooklyn, which

I also attended, and which is the locale for the WELCOME BACK, KOTTER TV series.

I secured Cornel Wilde's first screen test at RKO Pictures. I also arranged a screen test for a young, aspiring actor, John Freund, whom I had met when he wore an usher's uniform when he was the public address announcer at Ebbets Field in Brooklyn, whose job it was to identify the daffy Brooklyn Dodger beloved bums. We have remained good friends over the years. His name is now John Forsythe.

Schafer, promotional man for RCA Victor, shown with band leader, Tommy Dorsey, and radio personality, Ted Cott, at the RCA Victor plant in New Jersey.

Babe Ruth, when he was a Brooklyn Dodger coach, wi actor Jon Hall, who appeared in movies as Tarzan, a Schafer, who handled special promotion for the Brookl "Bums."

Arctic explorers Rear Admiral Richard E. Byrd and Sir Hubert Wilkins who was the first to reach the North Pole in a submarine underwater expedition.

Golf's all-time great Gene Sarazen and Schafer who were guests of Lowell Thomas at his estate in Pawling, New Yo

Movie comedian Joe E. Brown was introduced by Bill Leonard of CBS as "starving in 'Harvey' on Broadway."

Movie actress Fay Wray who earned lasting fame for her role in the original KING KONG movie.

The legendary tap dancing star "Bo Jangles," Bill Robinson, appearing on a Schafer-produced radio program.

LUNCHEON AT SARDI'S on Radio from famous Sardi's restaurant in New York. On left is movie actor John Garfield; on right is program host Bill Slater with his guest Mickey Schafer.

Wild animal adventurer Frank Buck of "Bring 'Em Back Alive" fame.

Movie cowboy star Hoot Gibson, who was represented by Schafer.

EARLY TELEVISION AN HISTORIC TV EVENT

I had the distinction of producing the first
television special ever on NBC-TV in the early
Blooper-filled days of TV. I clearly recall this
pioneering event when there were 200 small-
screen television sets in existence which produced
mostly "ghosts." I was given a budget of
$300 by NBC to pay a cast of 40 performers.
Only one camera was used to cover this video
disaster during which one of the girl dancers'
hair began to smolder because of the brutally
hot lights. I recall, too, the grotesque silver faces
and purple lips that were applied to the performers
by a befuddled make up department. I consider
myself accident prone which could have very
well motivated my involvement with Bloopers and
my empathy for Blooper victims. I belatedly
received a TV Guide Gold Medal Award for this
memorable television first.

TV GUIDE GOLD MEDAL AWARD

TV's FIRST SPECIAL
NBC-TV

kermit schafer
PRESENTS
TV BABES OF 1939

starring RAY HEATHERTON

starring JUNE HAVOC

ORIGINAL "FLIP" CARDS
which were set on easels
and flipped by hand
in early-day television.
This practice was followed
before the introduction
of slides for titles.

A CAST OF 40

TOTAL BUDGET: $300

338 CARNATION AVENUE
FLORAL PARK, LONG ISLAND

January 23, 1940

Mr. Schafer
N.B.C.
Rockefeller Plaza
New York City

Mr. Schafer:

Sunday night we were surprised to see on our new television some of our own people. It was wonderful. Came over very clearly. Ray Heatherton is the town favorite. He looked wonderful. So did all the performers. Called in all neighbors to see them. Wish all continued success and thanks for the talent. So nice to see some one we know. It was a good, enjoyable show.

Daisy Fitzsimmons

PRO-107 4-39

NATIONAL BROADCASTING COMPANY, INC.

PROGRAM DEPARTMENT

Sustaining Program Contract

Agreement dated January 8 , 19 40, between National Broadcasting Company, Inc., of 30 Rockefeller Plaza, New York, N. Y., hereinafter called "NBC," and _____

_____ Kermit K Schafer _____

whose address is Roger White Productions Inc., RKO Bldg., Rockefeller Center
hereinafter called "Artist."

NBC employs Artist, who accepts such employment, to render artistic services as follows:

Program Title: Original Babes of "Babes in Arms" - Television

Place and time of broadcast: New York City ____ from 8:30 P.M. to 9:30 P.M.
        (city)   (hour)

Sunday, January 21, 1940
(month, day, and year)

Additional broadcasts: _____

Fee: $300.00 $300.00

Other terms: Includes Cast, Music and dramatic rights and musical accompaniment.

_____

_____

Artist will be advised by the Production Division of NBC when and where to report for rehearsal. If this contract requires Artist to furnish material for his performance, he shall submit same to the Program Department of NBC as far as possible in advance of the date of broadcast. The additional provisions on the reverse side hereof are a part of this contract.

If this contract is made for the Artist by his duly authorized agent, such agent must sign in this space:
Artist:

By Same
DULY AUTHORIZED AGENT OF ARTIST

Address of agent is 270 6th Ave City

NATIONAL BROADCASTING COMPANY, INC.

By Thos H Hutchinson
      Kermit K Schafer
             ARTIST

Artist's Social Security No. is _____

One copy of this contract is to be returned promptly to NBC. Artist must sign, or his agent indicate, the name under which the Artist is registered with the Social Security Board and give the Social Security Number of the Artist.

ORIGINAL PAYMENT VOUCHERS

AUD. 7

NATIONAL BROADCASTING COMPANY, INC.

BELOW IS A STATEMENT OF TAXABLE EARNINGS COVERED BY THIS REMITTANCE AND THE FEDERAL OLD AGE BENEFITS TAX WHICH HAS BEEN DEDUCTED THEREFROM.

NAME	TAXABLE EARNINGS	FEDERAL OLD AGE BENEFITS TAX	DATE OF PAYMENT
Ray Heatherton (pd to Kermit K Schafer)	25.00	.25	2/1/40

Ray Heatherton

AUD. 7

NATIONAL BROADCASTING COMPANY, INC.

BELOW IS A STATEMENT OF TAXABLE EARNINGS COVERED BY THIS REMITTANCE AND THE FEDERAL OLD AGE BENEFITS TAX WHICH HAS BEEN DEDUCTED THEREFROM.

NAME	TAXABLE EARNINGS	FEDERAL OLD AGE BENEFITS TAX	DATE OF PAYMENT
June Havoc	$20.00	.20	2/1/40
Payment authorized by			

Kermit Schafer, PRODUCER
Edward Padula, DIRECTOR

MILITARY SERVICE

Schafer was fortunate to have been able to apply his theatrical talents in the military where he was an Entertainment Director in Special Services. He produced soldier shows in addition to radio programs featuring G.I.'s. Even at this early date he was fascinated with Blooper outtakes of G.I. training films which in many cases were hurriedly put together by inexperienced personnel who were assigned to the motion picture division of the Air Force. Among memorabilia that he has brought back from World War II are outtakes from training films which can be seen on his Blooper TV Specials.

Ezra Stone, radio's "Henry Aldrich," welcomes Schafer into military service.

Prior to entering the military service, Schafer represented the Special Events Division of the United States Treasury Department. He is shown with Hollywood star Olivia de Haviland at a War Bond Rally at Lewisohn Stadium in New York. Schafer accompanied Hollywood stars coast to coast in connection with the War Bond effort.

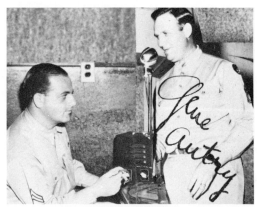

Cowboy singing star Staff Sergeant Gene Autry performing on a Schafer-produced radio program at Love Field Air Force Base in Dallas, Texas.

Veteran CBS sportscaster Ted Husing who was the commentator of radio's CHEERS FROM THE CAMPS which originated from Pine Camp, New York. Schafer produced the soldier portion of the broadcast.

Bette Davis, christening a P-38 fighter plane during a Stage Door Canteen Night produced by Schafer in Hollywood and tied-in with the CBS STAGE DOOR CANTEEN network radio program.

AFTER THE WAR

Schafer worked with Allen Funt, a boyhood buddy from the Borough Park section of Brooklyn. He sold Funt's CANDID MIKE series to Columbia Pictures for movie shorts and also produced Funt's hilarious CANDID MIKE record album. He attributes Funt as the chief motivating factor in the development of his Blooper collection which initially was a hobby. Many people in broadcasting, as well as Blooper fans, seem to draw a parallel between Funt's and Schafer's works. The difference is that CANDID CAMERA sets up "Bloopers" made by unsuspecting victims whereas Schafer's Bloopers are spontaneous.

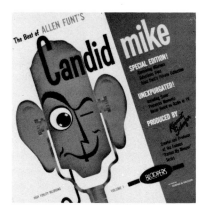

The back of the CANDID MIKE record album contains some amusing "liner" notes which describes Funt thusly. "Funt spent many years studying to be a spy at the Mata Hari Institute for Secret Agents. At good old "MHISA" he majored in such subjects as snooping, peeping, secret document swallowing, and inconscpicuosity. In this day of 'wiretaps,' he has graced some of the finest post offices in the country. His appearance, on many occasions, has been accompanied by the immortal words ... 'That's him, boys! Get him!'

Funt has recorded most of his sound on tape. Curiously enough, Kermit Schafer, the producer of this recording, also worked extensively with tape on his now famous PARDON MY BLOOPER albums. Both Schafer and Funt attended the same school and grew up to be 'tape-worms' together."

Bess Myerson, former Miss America, represented by Schafer, and Allen Funt of CANDID CAMERA fame and boyhood friend from Brooklyn.

The **CANDID MIKE** record album, which features the best of Allen Funt's CANDID MIKE radio series, preserves some of the classic moments of the popular radio program of the 1940's.

THE WRESTLER: An unsuspecting wrestler confided to Funt as to how all professional wrestling matches were faked. Funt hires him to wrestle him and to throw the match so that Funt can look good before a group of his friends. This was recorded by Funt as the risk of his life and limb.

THE SHOE SALESMAN: After helping a lady customer try on several pairs of shoes, Funt hid one of her shoes and insisted that she had come in the store with only one on. He drove the unsuspecting customer "bananas" while she tried to convince Funt that she most certainly did come in with two shoes. He tried to calm her down when he offered her a second left shoe "compliments of the store."

THE MOVER: A man came to move a trunk from which he heard moaning and groaning noises which Funt insisted the truckman imagined. In great fear, the mover said, "Here's your $20 back. Go find yourself another truckman."

CHAINED: A locksmith was called to Funt's office to saw off the chains from his secretary who Funt described as a "clock watcher" and who, he complained, left her job early every day. Funt said that he had lost the key to the lock. As the infuriated locksmith sawed away, Funt asked him how many similar situations he had encountered. The indignant locksmith replied, "Are you kidding? Nobody locks up his secretary. And they'd better not try!"

BLUE PLATE SPECIAL: Funt drives a busy waiter out of his mind by asking for substitutes, such as vegetables, which the waiter insists cannot be made. The waiter is ready to throw Funt out of the restaurant when Funt asks him to separate the peas, corn, and carrots which are part of the mixed vegetables.

FRUIT PEDDLER: Funt frustrates an Italian fruit peddler by sampling all of his fruits. After the tasting is done, Funt starts to leave. The irate street peddler asks, "Aren't you going to buy anything?" Funt answers, "No, I was just looking," to which the livid peddler screams, "Next time don't look with the mouth!"

TV PRODUCER

Kermit Schafer became a full-time producer of television programming in 1948 when he produced the initial programming at the opening of WPIX, Channel 11, in New York, which is owned by the New York DAILY NEWS. One of his long-running weekly programs was the RUBE GOLDBERG SHOW, a program of cartoon charades. It was on this program that Bennett Cerf, author and raconteur, appeared as a panelist for the first time and on which he uttered the first of his now legendary, outrageous puns on TV when he asked, "Did you hear about the cow who swallowed a bottle of ink and mooed indigo?"

Schafer with his production staff at WPIX studios, the New York DAILY NEWS TV station.

Sonny Tufts???, Hollywood film actor and the butt many jokes, with Candy Jones, former Conover mo and radio commentator, appearing on YOUR LUCI STAR, a Schafer-produced TV program on WPIX

Cartoonist Rube Goldberg, Pulitzer Prize winner, signing a contract for appearances as emcee on the Schafer-produced RUBE GOLDBERG SHOW. Goldberg was also known for his celebrated "Rube Goldberg goofy inventions."

Bennett Cerf in his first TV panel show appeara which preceded WHAT'S MY LINE?, and Dia Barrymore, actress daughter of movie star Jc Barrymore.

Schafer produced several TV programs on NBC's flagship station, WNBT, in New York, for many national advertisers, such as RCA, Westinghouse, Motorola, Bendix, Crosley, International Harvester, and other major sponsors. It was on one of his produced shows for Westinghouse that the classic Blooper occurred when Betty Furness attempted to open a locked refrigerator door. This memorable moment is shown in his BLUNDERFUL WORLD OF BLOOPERS TV Special.

CHANNEL 4 **WNBT**
more and more . . . . it's
NBC TELEVISION

Faye Emerson, the Queen of TV, with her bridegroom, Skitch Henderson, at their wedding reception. Schafer gave Henderson his first job as a TV personality.

Former movie actress Betty Furness whose legendary Westinghouse "stuck" refrigerator door occurred on Schafer's produced program.

"Uncle Milty," the King of TV, when he appeared on Schafer's produced NBC-TV TALENT SEARCH program.

PRODUCER OF TALENT SHOWS

Famed humorist Harry Hershfield, TALENT SEARCH emcee, shown with Schafer and sponsors.

Pianist-conductor Skitch Henderson who took over as emcee of TALENT SEARCH, and Maggie McNellis, early TV personality.

Unfortunately, all Bloopers are not funny. They sometimes border on the tragic. One such classic example occurred on a TV program that I produced on NBC which was known as TALENT SEARCH which featured non-professional talent, and which was sponsored by RCA Victor in cooperation with the Vim chain of retail stores selling the RCA product. When I chose Harry Hershfield to be emcee of the program, I, as well as the sponsor and NBC, had high hopes that Hershfield, a great humorist, raconteur, cartoonist of the newspaper syndicated cartoon "Abie Kabibble" for many years, would be a natural to compete with the Arthur Godfrey TALENT SCOUTS on the rival CBS-TV. During this period Hershfield was also feted as a great humanitarian.

Came the auspicious, black-tie premiere of this new, potentially exciting TV program of the 1950 season which originated from the International Theatre in midtown Manhattan, and which used the same audience that was used by Sid Caeser and the SHOW OF SHOWS. I felt that I had a sure winner ... until for some unexplainable reason Harry in an interview with a young pianist, who identified himself as Ed Spencer, exploded a bombshell. Spencer, who appeared to be of Hebrew extraction was shaken when Hershfield said, "Spencer ... I hope you'll be successful enough to go back to your right name." A hush fell upon the audience. As a result, the program fell apart with cues being missed, wrong talent being introduced to the accompaniment of wrong music by the orchestra, the program's running considerably over, and other disasters. The day after the calamity, newspapers blasted Hershfield for his bad taste and poor judgment. It was ironic for he had always been a model of discretion and a man of impeccible character who got caught up in a new and exacting media unlike radio where he was a panelist on IT PAYS TO BE IGNORANT. I was given the unpleasant task of removing Hershfield from the program after only one appearance.

Matters were made worse by an iron-clad contract that I had with Harry, the sponsors, and the network which was drawn up by our mutual attorney, famed and brilliant lawyer Louis Nizer. As I look back on it now, Hershfield's breach by today's standards would be considered minor what with all of the sick religious, irreverent barbs being bantered about nightly on the tube.

MISS U.S. TV TV'S FIRST BEAUTY PAGEANT

Schafer shown selecting contestants for the Miss U.S. TV Contest, the forerunner of many TV beauty and talent contests which followed.

Briefing the Miss U.S. TV Contest judges: Harry Conover, New York model impressario; Ham Fisher, cartoonist of "Joe Palooka"; and Danton Walker New York DAILY NEWS Columnist.

Schafer who was a judge in the Miss Florida competition as part of the Miss America TV pageant.

Beauty pageants on TV, such as Miss America, Miss Universe, and Miss World, have become a tradition largely as a result of the huge audiences they attract which are reflected in the ratings. They are presented live, and as a result, the contestants, as well as other participants in the festivities, are under a great strain and are understandably nervous. On the Miss U.S. Television program, TV's first beauty pageant contest that I produced in New York in association with Walter Schwimmer of Chicago and telecast on NBC-TV in 1951, many Bloopers occurred.

Ham Fisher, creator of the cartoon character, Joe Palooka, and one of the judges, committed what he later admitted was a Freudian slip. When he was introduced to millions of TV viewers, he blooped, "With all the beauty here tonight, I want to grasp for breast . . . I mean, GASP FOR BREATH!"

Edie Adams, first winner of the Miss U.S. TV Contest, congratulating her successor.

PANEL SHOWS

QUICK ON THE DRAW was a forerunner of the many game shows which followed. I produced this show on three TV stations over a ten-year-period, commencing in the mid-forties, on WPIX, NBC, and WABD, the Dumont television station named after Dr. Allen B. Dumont, the television pioneer whose company made the first electronic receiver sold in the United States. This program of cartoon charades, which was patterned after the age-old charades parlor game, orginated from the John Wanamaker's department store studio in downtown New York. This was the antiquated location for such now-legendary programs as CAPTAIN VIDEO. Dumont also carried the original JACKIE GLEASON SHOW which featured the successful "Honeymooners."

Rube Goldberg, one of America's best-known cartoonists, who was the first emcee of QUICK ON THE DRAW, a program of cartoon charades.

Bob Dunn, King Features' syndicated cartoonist and President of the National Cartoonist Society, inherited QUICK ON THE DRAW from Rube Goldberg.

French movie actress Denise Darcel, center, with Eloise McElhone, QUICK ON THE DRAW co-emcee on NBC, and who was the loquacious member of NBC-TV's LEAVE IT TO THE GIRLS panel show.

Veteran actor Walter Abel presenting award to Schafer and Robin Chandler, who emceed QUICK ON THE DRAW on Dumont, for their efforts on behalf of retarded children. Chandler is the wife of Angie Biddle Duke, Chief of Protocol during the Kennedy Administration.

Movie character actor Guy Kibee; "The Great Dunninger," TV mentalist who used his "powers" to guess the answers.

Left to right: Schafer, Democratic party head and Postmaster General James Farley, movie actress Virginia Field, Met opera star Helen Jepson, and Restaurateur Toots Shor in a briefing session.

Schafer briefing celebrity contestants on his QUICK ON THE DRAW program of cartoon charades. Listening intently are the husband-and-wife team of Tex and Jinx, Tex McCrary and Jinx Falkenberg, and celebrated party-giver, Elsa Maxwell.

Are Panel and Quiz Shows Honest or Phony?

Kermit Schafer has produced several quiz and game shows. He was the first to "blow the whistle" on dishonest programs on which valuable prizes were offered. In a United Press interview he told UP correspondent Bill Ewald, "You just can't run a panel or quiz show without some planted answers and ad libs." This provocative article caused a furor in television, with indignant replies from Dorothy Kilgallen of WHAT'S MY LINE, Gene Raeburn, Fred Allen, who became a TV panelist, and others. It was soon after that the $64,000 QUESTION TV scandal shocked the nation.

Schafer recalls, "One time I had Tony Canzoneri, the former world's lightweight boxing champion, on one of my panel shows. It was a program of cartoon clues, and I told him before the show that one of the answers was ' poison ivy.' Well, the first clue was drawn. The correct answer was Henry Wadsworth Longfellow, but Tony shouted 'poison ivory!' He kept shouting 'poison ivory' for the first seven questions and was wrong every time. The whole show was falling apart, and I finally motioned him to be quiet. The next cartoon clue turned out to be a bottle of poison plus some ivy climbing up a wall. But Tony just sat there and never said a word."

TV contestant Charles Van Doren confessed to the House investigations that he was "deeply involved in a deception" when he won $129,000 on The $64,000 QUESTION.

We're celebrating the 25th year of producer Kermit Schafer's
BLUNdeRFUL WORLd OF BLooPeRs ©

Unbleeped Bloopers
BURT PRELUTSKY   *Reprinted from Los Angeles Times*

● The year 1952 doesn't seem so long ago until you realize that Truman was then President, there was a war going on in Korea, next to nobody had yet heard of Paul Newman, Elvis Presley, Arnold Palmer, Audrey Hepburn or a place called Vietnam, and Gunsmoke was still just the name of a radio show.

In the election of 1952, the team of Eisenhower and Nixon trounced Stevenson and Sparkman. Frank Sinatra's first comeback was still a year off, Martin and Lewis were still hanging together and Liz Taylor was only married to No. 2, Michael Wilding.

When you realize how drastically the world has changed, one way and another, during those past 22 years, the most amazing Kermit Schafer's accomplishment appears. For it was in 1952 that Schafer came up with the notion of collecting and marketing bloopers. When you think of all the fads that have come and gone during that period, it is astounding to realize that Schafer's brainstorm is still going strong after 30 record albums, a dozen books and, now, a movie, "Pardon My Blooper."

The first classic blooper is attributed to Harry Von Zell. In introducing our 31st President to a radio audience, Von Zell called him Hoobert Heever. The latest, according to Schafer, was the TV newscaster who attributed a Washington rumor to "high White Horse souses."

I asked Schafer how he had prepared himself for such a peculiar career. "I was a TV producer for many years. In fact, I produced TV's first full-hour musical for NBC. It starred Ray Heatherton and June Havoc, had a cast of 40 singers and dancers, and a total budget of $300.
Later, I did some work with Allen Funt. Also, I produced the Rube Goldberg Show in New York. It was on that show and not, as most people think, on Studio One, that Betty Furness did the famous Westinghouse commercial in which she couldn't open the refrigerator door."

I wondered if the fact that live TV is pretty much passe has made the blooper business more difficult. "Not really. I've had very good luck being able to latch on to out-takes. And because everything is taped or filmed, performers feel they can take greater liberties. They feel that if they goof or get tongue-tied, it can always be edited out."

I asked Schafer whether, 25,000 bloopers later, he was beginning to weary of the career he had carved out for himself back in '52. "Never. It's a great life. I help make people laugh and I make a very good living doing it. What more could a person want?" Fame?

But is it enough to have been the fellow who turned slips of the tongue into a profitable way of life? What, I asked Schafer, would he ultimately wish as his epitaph? "I never really gave it any thought. My credo, however, is: To forgive is human; to err, divine."

Let's face it, Schafer has gone on thriving long after such 1952 biggies as Pinky Lee, Korla Pandit, Johnny Ray and Julius La Rosa have been remaindered as trivia items. Bloopers have survived coonskin caps, blue suede shoes and even Tom Swifties. Of everything, in fact, that existed in 1952 the only things that remain basically unaltered and intact today, besides bloopers, are Alabama's Sen. John Sparkman, the American Legion, What's My Line? and David Cassidy's singing voice. Viewed from that perspective, Schafer's contribution to our culture and our society emerges as positively awe-inspiring.

THE ORIGINAL BLOOPER ALBUM

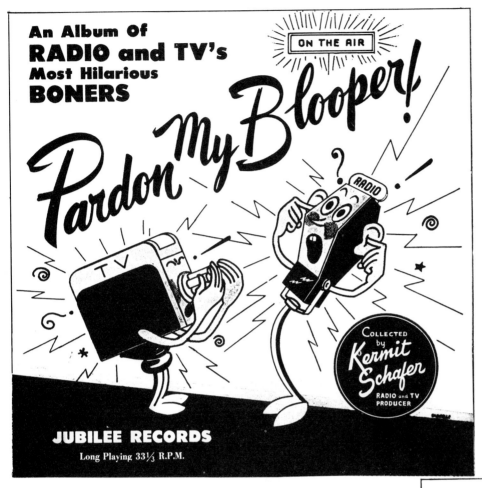

The now legendary front cover of PARDON MY BLOOPER, the first comedy LP ever and the first comedy million seller. The "Ike" and "Mike" logo, "Ike" standing for iconoscope and "Mike" for microphone, has become recognized internationally as a guarantee of a good laugh.

Inasmuch as Schafer has made Bloopers a full-time occupation, he zealously guards his copyrighted and trade-marked properties. The Supreme Court of the State of New York upheld him in a case where there was an unauthorized use of some of his material. An injunction was granted in his favor. Mr. Justice Di Falco, in his opinion in the Law Journal, stated, "... Such material as compiled by plaintiff was done in such a way as to make it a distinctive and unique format ..."

THE FIRST BLOOPER BOOK

The Cash Box
VOL. XXI—NO. 28 MARCH 26, 1960

Steve Allen, reading excerpts from YOUR SLIP IS SHOWING!, the first of several Blooper books, about which he says, "It catches Radio and TV with its Bloomers down . . . I mean, BLOOPERS!!!"

Jerry Blaine, President of Jubilee Records, presents Schafer with the record industry's first Gold Album for comedy.

SOURCES OF MATERIAL

An early photo showing Schafer with a stack of Blooper mail.

Schafer has made his Blooper works a national institution, and he has become a definitive authority and reporter on the subject. His internationally famous collection has become an integral part of the humor heritage of Americana. Mr. Blooper, as he has become affectionately known to his countless fans worldwide, has enlisted a dedicated network of watchdogs numbering millions of TV viewers and radio listeners from all walks of life which insures a steady flow of Blooper contributions which arrive daily at Blooper Head quarters in Miami, Florida. The material is sent in letters as well as in audio and video tape form.

RADIO-TV STATIONS

- ☐ PROGRAM DIRECTOR
- ☐ PUBLICITY DIRECTOR
- ☐ ENGINEERS
- ☐ ANNOUNCERS
- ☐ ACTORS
- ☐ DISK JOCKEYS
- ☐ COMMENTATORS
- ☐ SPORTSCASTERS
- ☐ RECORD LIBRARIAN

HOW BLOOPER RECORDS ARE MADE

MONITORING

Kermit Schafer shown monitoring audio tapes for Bloopers. These tapes have been transferred from ELECTRICAL TRANSCRIPTIONS, KINESCOPES, SOUNDTRACKS, VIDEO TAPES, OFF-THE-AIR RECORDINGS and other bona fide sources. A good portion of the Bloopers in his collection have been the result of his own monitoring system. The balance are from material sent to him from Blooper fans from all over the world.

CATALOGING

Shown is a portion of Schafer's tape library which contains his vast storage of Bloopers. Bloopers are filed under program categories such as QUIZ, SPORTS, MUSIC, KIDS, DRAMATIC, NEWS, etc. Bloopers are also filed under personnel categories such as ACTORS, ANNOUNCERS, DISC JOCKEYS, CELEBRITIES, etc. This valuable treasury of hilarious boners dates back from the early days of radio to modern-day television.

EDITING

One of Schafer's most tedious jobs is the task of editing his collection of Radio and Television Bloopers. His experienced and expert sense of timing and comedy insures a fast-moving and laugh-provoking series of recordings which now number more than thirty. The initial phase of editing is done in his own studio.

MASTERING

The final stage before a Blooper album is pressed is Mastering. A master recording is processed from the completely edited master tape, from which metal stampers are made. These stampers or plates press the thousands of recordings which are distributed throughout the world.

THE SCHAFER HOME AND LISTENING POST
IN UPSTATE NEW YORK

Photos by EZRA STOLLER

Inside McCall's
BLOOPERS
MONTHLY FEATURE

High on a hill overlooking the Ramapo Mountains in Central Valley, New York, sits a modern redwood house which is the home of Radio-TV producer Kermit Schafer. This attractive and interesting home, which has been featured in such national magazines as McCALL's, has become a veritable listening post for Radio and TV Bloopers.

On a visit inside, you will see a battery of built-in tape recorders which are constantly in operation in the process of monitoring several programs simultaneously. This equipment doesn't interfere with the convenience of modern living as it is all functionally built in to go with the rest of the modern furnishings. With all of this equipment Kermit Schafer, or "Mr. Blooper," as he is sometimes referred to, capitalizes on the mistakes of others.

MAGNETIC FILM &
TAPE RECORDING

World's Leading Recording Magazine

EXCLUSIVE!

TAPE RECORDING RADIO AND TV BLOOPERS

•

THE INSIDE STORY OF KERMIT SCHAFER'S FAMOUS BLOOPER COLLECTION

•

TAPE RECORDERS

LISTENING POST

BLOOPERS INC.
BLOOPER ALBUMS
BOOKS
SYNDICATED COLUMN
MERCHANDISING
BLOOPERAMA
ETC.

Radio-TV Producer Kermit Schafer's Blooper Listening Post

THE BLOOPER STORY, reprinted from Tape Recording Magazine   35c

The Schafers shown on their mountain top terrace monitoring tapes for Bloopers which were recorded on several tape recorders tuned into several Radio and TV stations.

Kermit Schafer's personal life is a quiet and private one. He has his own studio whether it be in the secluded mountain top retreat in upstate New York or the beauty of the tropical surroundings of his home in south Florida. He pursues his hobby, golf, with his pretty wife, Mickey who is a low 3 handicap amateur golfer who played on the national amateur tour. Their celebrated One-Hole Golf Course has been featured on the cover of the NATIONAL GOLFER and has resulted in many well-known professional and amateur golfers visiting the unique golf hole. President Eisenhower paid the Schafers an unannounced and unpublicized visit to take a brief look at the golf hole when he was in Central Valley attending an annual West Point reunion held at restauranteur Gene Leone's farm close to the Schafer property. The President, an ardent golfer, had written him after receiving an honorary membership in the One-Hole Country Club, in which he said, "Concerning the One-Hole Golf Course you and Mrs. Schafer have on the grounds surrounding your home in Central Valley, even the putting green at Gettysburg can't begin to compete with the fun of having one complete hole on which to practice all kinds of shots." When Schafer moved his Blooper Headquarters to the Coral Gables area of Florida, his home and acreage were bought by Benihana, the Japanese restauranteur family, who built their Gasho village and restaurant on his property.

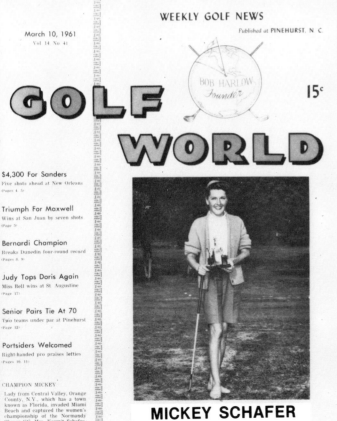

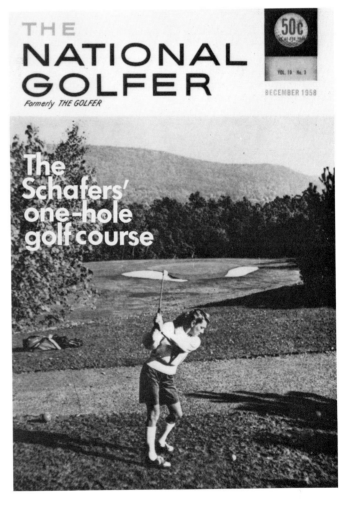

THE SCHAFER HOME IN SOUTH FLORIDA

The Schafer home is a contemporary structure located in the historic Old Cutler Road area of Miami, Florida. It is surrounded by prize-winning landscaping which offers a total seclusion which is conducive for the concentration needed for his many and varied Blooper projects. A separate building, which he uses as a studio, is located near his Coral Gables offices which are the headquarters of Blooper Enterprises, Inc.

A Coca-Cola TV commercial being filmed on the grounds of the Schafer residence. Shown are the McCann-Erickson advertising representatives and the production crew.

A view of the Schafer tennis court during the filming of the TV commercial.

VISITORS TO THE SCHAFER HOME

Schafer has a host of good friends from all walks of the entertainment industry. They, too, are among his loyal fans. They are quick to take advantage of his hospitality at his home where they are also treated to the pleasure of listening to some of his private Blooper collection.

Bob Merrill, composer of FUNNY GIRL and many other hits; Schafer; actor Jose Ferrer; and George Roy Hill, movie director and producer of BUTCH CASSIDY AND THE SUNDANCE KID and THE STING.

Henny Youngman, King of the one-liners.

Milton Berle enjoying a Blooper album.

Stage and movie actor Richard Conte who was a wartime GI buddy of Schafer.

SOME OF THE SCHAFERS' FRIENDS

"Muffin" (as in muffing lines).

"Mr. Blooper," thoroughbred race horse.

"Fluffin" (as in fluffing lines).

SPEECH MASTERS PROFESSORS OF THE CLYDE

Al Kelly, Master of Double-talk, who made a career out of confusing millions of listeners with his unique jargon, cooking up some "leg pulling" on a visit to Schafer's home.

Norm Crosby, Master of the Malaprop, who made a career out of "murdering" the King's English, getting some ideas from actual Bloopers for his successful act.

I had the great fortune to know Al Kelly, a genius in the art of double-talk and who has amused and confused millions including world celebrities who have been his victims. I derived a great deal of fun from his put-ons, so much that I have produced a TV Special entitled THE PRANKSTERS which features classic hoaxes perpetrated in broadcasting.

In one classic example, Kelly was speaking to a distinguished group in the medical profession. Looking like a physician himself and in serious tones, he addressed the group. "Good evening, I should like to dwell tonight upon the postoperative aspect of brain surgery, with especial reference to the occipital region as distinguished from the parietal. Those of you who are familiar with my work in Egypt and Tibet on these portions of the human brain will recognize that there is a difference in the techniques involved in a thrave that has no froyd when the krauman is preceded by a throll ..." The doctors were awed because he slipped in words like "thrave," "krauman," and "throll" so quickly and earnestly that they blamed their confusion on a noise in the room or a cough somewhere. Some worried doctor in the crowd, who heard them clearly, admitted later that he made a mental note to look them up when he got home.

Kelly was known for his antics off stage as well as on. Here is an example revolving around lunch with Jackie Gleason at Toot Shor's when a waiter took his order. "Bring me a glave with a hot blye." The waiter eyed him, but before he could ask him what he said, Kelly continued, "Be sure it's hot. Then have the chef make me a bleaven, fried lightly, with clades, brule, and cryne, but no onions. Put the

brule on a separate plate. Okay?" While the waiter was trying to compose himself, Gleason said, "I'll take the same."

Allen Funt, with whom I have worked over the years, has been the Master of the Put-ons as evidenced by his long-running CANDID MIKE and CANDID CAMERA series. From time to time he has used celebrity "needlers" as foils such as the time he enlisted the services of Al Kelly. The scene was a paint store where Funt posed as owner. Kelly was hidden in another room. A lady walked into the store, approaching Funt who was on the phone at the counter.

"I wonder if I could ask a favor of you, madam. I have a man on the phone who wants to give me a very big order, but I can't seem to understand him. Would you please help me get the order?"

"Why, of course," said the lady obligingly as Funt gave her the phone.

"Look, I'm getting a little tired of this. If somebody doesn't take my order right now, I can find a store that will."

"No, no, give it to me, I've got the order form..."

"I want a three-quarter gallon of orange frytken floyden, a single esterup of blay, and the brushes must be doyne, but with a fahn."

"Talk slowly, please," said the lady, "I'm writing it down."

Kelly gave her the order again while Funt had difficulty in controlling himself.

"Would you mind repeating that again?"

"A three-quarter gallon of orange frytken floyden

In a state of confusion, she asked, "How do you spell orange?"

THE BLOOPER CHAMP

Ed Sullivan in a typical introduction blooped, "Sitting out in our audience is talented Dolores Gray currently starving on Broadway."

Vincent Sardi, Jr., famed restaurateur, who displayed BLUNDERFUL WORLD OF BLOOPERS in his showcase of theatrical books. Schafer was associated with the LUNCHEON AT SARDI'S Radio and TV talk show program.

In my many Radio and TV guest appearances, as well as before the public, one question is invariably asked of me. "Who has committed the most Bloopers?" Ed Sullivan has got to be the Champion of Live TV and Johnny Carson, the King of the Talk Shows. Carson is listed in my BLUNDERFUL WORLD OF BLOOPERS book index 27 times.

In the early days of the ED SULLIVAN SHOW, I was called upon to help fill his audience with celebrities. At that time I had performed the same function for LUNCHEON AT SARDI's radio program on the Mutual Network which originated from the famous Sardi's theatrical restaurant in New York. Some of my celebrity panel shows were aired on Sunday night preceding the ED SULLIVAN SHOW. I would, therefore, "shuttle" my celebrity guests by taxi to the theatre where Ed's show originated. In the few short minutes I had with him, I had to brief him about the celebrities. What usually followed was a disaster, such as the time he introduced swimming champions and movie stars Buster Crabbe and Johnny Weismuller as having been inducted into the "Swimming Hole of Fame." Of course, he meant "Swimming Hall of Fame." On another occasion, Ed introduced a group of dentists who attended a Dental Convention in New York City and who were his guests in the theatre audience. Later in the program he introduced a Polish dance group thusly. "And now on our stage, we have a marvelous group of performers . . . 40 Polish dentists!!"

Poor Ed. His background as a columnist for the New York DAILY NEWS was not enough to cope with the murderous rigors of live TV. I can recall when I was packaging a series of movie shorts featuring screen tests of aspiring actors, Ed came to see me in my office in the RKO Building in Radio City, New York. I had him read a few lines after which I politely told him to stick to his column. Some years later, during the course of a LUNCHEON AT SARDI's radio program, Marlo Lewis sat down at a table where I was sitting with Sid Weiss of RADIO-TV DAILY and Gary Stevens, publicist and columnist, all of whom had an interest in the SARDI's program. Marlo announced, "I just came from CBS. They have signed Ed Sullivan to emcee a talent-variety show which I am to produce.

"Ed Sullivan on live network TV??!!" I shook my head in disbelief. In my mind I could imagine the Bloopers. Perhaps, unconsciously, this was prophetic as it had a bearing on my future.

A group of producers waiting to be "shuttled" to the ED SULLIVAN SHOW. Left to right: Brock Pemberton, Broadway stage producer; Kermit Bloomgarten, producer of DEATH OF A SALESMAN; Jean Dalrymple, PORGY AND BESS; and Leo McCarey, director of GOIN' MY WAY.

MASTERS OF THE ADLIB CELEBRITY ROASTS

I have had the privilege to present my Blooper program before theatrical organizations, such as the Footlighters Club in Miami Beach, which is the counterpart of the celebrated Friars Club in New York. In the course of these appearances, I was given a precious tape which was literally smuggled out of a Masquers' dinner roasting veteran movie producer Harry Joe Brown on the West Coast. Theatrical groups had an ironclad law banning any recording of their festivities which were considered very private. Unlike the watered-down, pre-written Dean Martin TV Roasts, the all male participants "let their hair down" with hilarity the main goal. Many years have lapsed since this classic display of humor which, although sprinkled with profanity, is primarily meant to be funny, not vulgar. In the spirit of preserving the brilliance of the extemporaneous performances by show business greats, and with the new acceptance by the largely liberal-minded public at this point in time, here are excerpts from the actual "Roast." George Jessel, the Toastmaster General of the world and who is without peer, is the "Roastmaster" of this classic event.

Schafer appearing at a Footlighters Club luncheon, Miami Beach, with "Roastee" movie actor Brian Donlevy and Footlighters' President and comedian Paul Gray.

JESSEL: In the last ten years I have probably made more public addresses and speeches than all my contemporaries put together. And because of this and because I speak in the next 90 days, I speak in 80 cities, I am called upon to prepare a manuscript for every place that I go. Just a short time ago I spoke in Detroit to the Knights of Columbus and addressed them as Gentlemen of the B'nai Brith. Therefore, I have several notes here, and I wear this glass not for any thought of being affected in any way, but I have trouble with this eye. And I would rather have people say, "Isn't he eccentric," than "the poor son of a bitch is going blind." I am glad that I am finding these impromptu things because I brought with me a speech for a circumcision in Glendale. I shall bravely bring this courtier of speakers to the microphone including our guest of honor. Someone gave me as a key in presenting him which I shall do later by saying he is such a man much as Will Rogers was. He never met a man that he didn't like. I don't find this any great virtue. I also had a wife who never met a man she didn't like ... I bring now to the microphone the luckiest straight man who ever lived in God's world. He did a vaudeville act, and while working in the Nagasaki Japanese troupe, he was known as Abe Stern. I present to you, Mr. George Burns.

BURNS: Thank you, Georgie, and Harry Joe Brown. I really should be in bed. I just got through doing a television show, and we filmed this in one day. I am so tired and exhausted that I probably won't remember one line that I'm supposed to adlib tonight. When they told me that I would have to speak tonight, even though it's shooting day, I couldn't turn it down because Harry and I have been friends all our lives. We have sort've been brought up together, we've had good times together; we've had bad times together; As a matter of fact we both got a touch of cupid's eczema from the same girl together. That was some girl ... Trixie Hicks. Four days later I limped into Dr. Milikson's office, and I saw Harry there. And I said, "Harry, what are you doing here?" He says, "I got a bad throat." The doctor said, "Take down your pants, I'd like to look at it." This was some office. After about four months, I got to know every actor by his ass.

But I've got to tell you a little story about Harry Joe. Harry and I were living at the Coolidge Hotel. He was going around with a girl then called Gladys Trueblood. She lived on the third floor, and Harry lived on the ninth. Sometimes he'd go downstairs to see her, and then he would come up. Sometimes she'd come up to see him and then go down. Sometimes she'd come up, and he'd go down. Sometimes they both went down. Once when he was down there, he ran into Lou Holtz. Must have been a Friday night 'cause Harry told me he wore his hat. This affair didn't last too long. Gladys Trueblood went back to Oklahoma City, and Harry went back to have his throat treated. Then Harry left for the coast and got mixed up with Charles Rogers, and they went into the picture business. And Charlie was telling me how Harry got his first money. It seems that Harry invented a machine that they used in Alaska, and this machine made a fortune for him. The miners up there would want a woman and couldn't get any so they would settle for some Eskimo woman. When they were finished, they would put a half dollar in Harry's machine, and it would defrost their balls. I told Charlie that's not true; that's a lie. He took off his pants and showed me a scar where he had gotten one of his balls caught in the machine. Anyway, Harry, I am very happy to be here tonight to say all these nice things about you.

JESSEL: In my new book, THIS WAY, MISS, I will lament that the TV and radio has done so little to bring forth any real talent. In a forthcoming one, I have already made a series of notes in regard to a fine and handsome product in this newest, shall I say, of the arts. May God forgive me for lying . . . Mr. Art Linkletter.

LINKLETTER: A long and lengthy and very literate wire arrived from the Harlequin inviting me to be here, and I was very pleased to be invited except for one small word which I knew would be in the wire and that is that it would be stag. Now in spite of what Mr. Jessel has told you about my seeming complacency and calm in front of an audience, you don't realize what happens to a man of of my background and character when I am invited to speak at a stag dinner where I know that I am going to be preceded by George Burns and George Jessel. I come from the type of show business where clean living, good thinking, most of the audience is born in wedlock. To get into the mood to come down to talk to you here in the vein which you enjoy requires at least three or four days of Jekyll and Hyde type preparation, starting on Monday, down at CBS television, going into the men's room and writing dirty words on the wall. On Tuesday I knew I was getting into the mood when my children came down for breakfast, and I called them all little sons of bitches. This morning, purely adlib, I phoned my mother-in-law in San Diego and told her to go fuck herself. When this happened, I knew I was ready for tonight.

JESSEL: In presenting your next speaker this evening, it is most easy to hurl superlatives in his direction. I know of nothing else to say to you except I know no man who holds a higher place in the hearts and affections of people of America and those of the amusement world, Mr. Jack Benny.

BENNY: You know when you have to follow fellows like Jessel, George Burns, and Linkletter, you get that completely sunk feeling as if you left your script in Milton Berle's dressing room. I don't know why I'm always asked to speak late at these stag dinners. I guess the only word left for me tonight is fornicate. You know I tried that once when I had to speak very late at a Friars' stag party, and I used the word fornicate, there was nothing else left, and I used it in a joke, and unfortunately, no one at the Friars understood what it meant except Ronald Reagan. Then I found out that when I used the word, it wasn't that they didn't understand it, it was that they didn't hear it because of all the dirty stuff. By the time I got on, all the Friars were playing with themselves. At the next banquet they had shorter tablecloths. Incidentally, I went to a party for Noel Coward Sunday; everyone tries to act so British. There was one dame there riding a Kotex side-saddle. I made a few notes myself because like Jessel I have to speak very, very often. I speak almost as often as Jessel, not quite as much, but I've never spoken at a circumcision, of course. I just cried at mine. But when I was asked to speak here tonight, I was very, very hesitant about coming, gentlemen, because although I like Harry Joe Brown very much, and I have known him for years, I didn't feel that he was a character who is conducive to stag material. He isn't the type of shit heel you can poke fun at like say, I don't think he is a shit heel comparable to the others. Harry Joe Brown is the kind of fellow you don't associate with stag dinners. So I didn't want to come for that reason. Then I thought, well, I should come. And another reason I wanted to come was because I am the Abbott of the Friars which is a very important executive position there. I would say that the Abbott of the Friars is equivalent to a diaphragm for Christine Jorgenson.

GEORGE JESSEL

GEORGE BURNS

ART LINKLETTER

JACK BENNY

INSIDE TV

Johnny Carson reading excerpts from a Blooper book. Also shown are Ed McMahon and writer-comedienne Selma Diamond.

In an appearance with Johnny Carson on his NBC-TV TONIGHT SHOW, celebrating the 10th Anniversary of Bloopers, Johnny related his thoughts about Bloopers and live TV.

"I think this show and shows that work in front of a live audience are a lot more fun than filmed or taped shows because all of the goofs are now gone out of so many television shows. Whereas in the early days of television everything was practically live, and there were some of the greatest dramatic shows. Remember the old PLAYHOUSE 90? Those were the fun, the great ones to watch."

(AFTER PLAYING A RECORDING OF A LOWELL THOMAS' CLASSIC BREAKUP) "Oh, the agony. Unless you've been behind the microphone at any one time, it may be a little hard to appreciate that, but it's devastating. It's like laughing in church. It's the wrong place, and as you look back on it, there was nothing funny, but at the time you just absolutely come apart."

"They used to sit down on the floor before they had teleprompters. . . with idiot cards down low. It's kinda frightening to see yourself walking out there, and boy, you just think that you're slick as a whistle . . . In the early days you were scared to look anywhere but at the camera because they always kept saying 'Look into the camera.' That was the only instruction that they gave you in television. Don't make a move unless it's all preset. The lights used to be much hotter because in those days you had real, real hot lights, and you were supposed to look right at home."

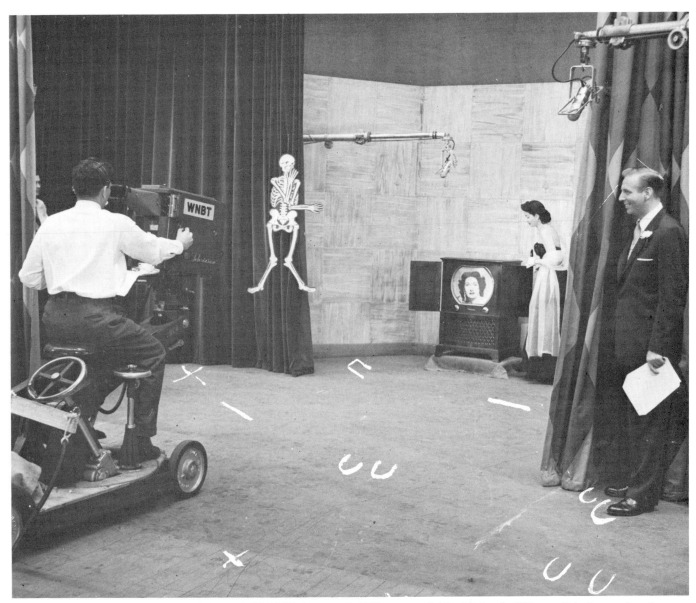

Skitch Henderson participating with Maggie McNellis in an early TV commercial for Motorola TV on a Schafer-produced TALENT SEARCH program on NBC. Shown are the various floor marks which conformed to preset camera shots.

"Idiot cards," large handprinted copy on poster boards, were used before the advent of the teleprompter.

The Teleprompter, a visual aid which revolutionized television for countless performers. The sophisticated, large moving type affords the user near-perfect and foolproof results.

SHOWS

Talk shows, in addition to the exposure of Blooperology to a nation-wide audience, afford me an opportunity to collect material from various guests, such as the British actor Michael York, who told me about the poor London announcer who was a victim of a "clanger," the British counterpart of the Blooper, who startled viewers with "This is BBC, the British Broadcorping Castration!"

Left to right: Comedienne Nancy Walker; Linda Hopkins, singing star of ME AND BESSIE; Reverend Jesse Jackson, Jr., civil rights activist; Dinah Shore; British actor Michael York; and Sch

Robert Goulet, center, tells of his Blooper when he forgot the words of "Star Spangled Banner" preceding a nationally televised heavyweight boxing championship from Las Vegas. Left to right: Vicki Lawrence, comedienne on the CAROL BURNETT SHOW; Mike Douglas; Goulet; Jon Voight, star of MIDNIGHT COWBOY; and Schafer.

160

TO TELL THE TRUTH

**WILL THE REAL KERMIT SCHAFER
PLEASE STAND UP?**

When I was invited to appear as a guest on the Goodson-Todman-produced TO TELL THE TRUTH, I accepted for the exposure which the program offered my Blooper properties. To his credit, Bill Cullen one of the program panelists, disqualified himself saying, "I have to disqualify myself because I have known and worked with Mr. Schafer over the years."

Panelists very often evoke some unpredictable Bloopers due to unplanned questions and answers. One such moment occurred when Panelist Peggy Cass asked me "Did our host, Mr. Moore, ever do anything naughty on the air . . . and is it true that he once did a dance with not all of his clothes buttoned up by mistake? Would that be considered a Blooper since it was a visual joke?"

MOORE: (INDIGNANTLY) A visual joke? I must say I have been injured deeply in my time, but I am wounded to the quick, and I have a very slow quick!

Needless to say . . . the audience howled at this double entendre.

Left to right: Emcee Garry Moore; Bill Cullen, radio and TV personality; and baseball pitching great Tom Seaver.

Singer-actress Kitty Carlisle.

Comedienne Peggy Cass.

THE BLOOPER AWARDS
AN ANNUAL TV EVENT
IN THE TRADITION OF
OSCAR...TONY...GRAMMY AND EMMY

The BLOOPER AWARDS is an annual TV Special on which the coveted Bloopy, the symbol of human error in broadcasting, is presented to the victims of Bloopers in all broadcast categories. I became the victim of a Freudian slip during an early BLOOPER AWARDS taping when a beautiful, buxom gal helped in awarding the Bloopy statuette. I blooped, "Our lovely Blooper Girl will assist in the presentation for broadcasting's breast Bloopers!"

THE BLOOPY AWARD

THE ENVELOPE

THE WINNERS ARE ...

On one of my many appearances on the MIKE DOUGLAS SHOW, Ted Knight was the co-host. I learned from him that he was a key figure in one of the most celebrated Bloopers in my collection. He told me on the air that he was the extra in the presentation of ABE LINCOLN IN ILLINOIS. The dramatic scene had Raymond Massey, who portrayed Lincoln, on the platform of railroad car surrounded by well-wishers who were bidding him a fond farewell. It was at this dramatic moment that Ted's voice could be heard above the milling crowd which was saying good bye. Ted blooped, "Good bye, Mr. Massey," which was heard by startled viewers. For his classic goof, I presented him with the coveted Blooper Award.

Ted Knight, who played the bumbling Ted Baxter on the long-running Mary Tyler Moore Show, receiving the Blooper Award.

MR. BLOOPER BLOOPS!! BLOOPERS UNIVERSAL

Larry King, Mutual Network radio personality.

A BBC disc jockey in London interviewing "Mr. Bloomer!"

I have been the victim of many a Blooper which has given me an empathy for other victims. In the pursuit of my unique Blooper career, spreading the Blooper gospel, I have appeared on many Radio and TV programs. A Freudian slip occurred in an appearance with Mutual Networks and Miami Radio and TV personality Larry King, who was extolling my Blooper accomplishments, when he asked, "Kermit, what is your credo?" Meaning to quote Alexander Pope, I replied, "To forgive is human, to err divine."

When I compiled my first book of Bloopers in 1953 published by Grayson and titled YOUR SLIP IS SHOWING, I became the victim of a typist's Blooper. I had been at my summer home in upstate Central Valley, New York, working on the book, and upon completion of the first draft, I hired a local typist to make a clean copy of the material and to make any corrections necessary before my mailing it to my publisher. I thought that this would be a good time to relax and play a round of golf with Nick Kenny, who was the Radio-TV columnist of the New York DAILY MIRROR and who was a house guest. After an enjoyable day at the nearby Central Valley Golf Course, I returned to check what appeared to be a neatly typed manuscript. I did a double-take when I picked up a page on which newsman and WHAT'S MY LINE? emcee John Daly's Blooper appeared. John Daly had written the Foreword to YOUR SLIP IS SHOWING, and I wanted to be doubly sure that the Blooper he furnished me was completely accurate. His Blooper was "Representative Spit smoked to you from Washington." I couldn't believe it . . . she corrected it to "Representative Smith spoke to you from Washington." She had corrected all of the Bloopers!!

I recall in an interview on BBC, in London when I became the victim of a British Disc Jockey's "Clanger" (Blooper). In a politeness typical of the British, he did not want to appear ignorant about Bloopers, which at the time were virtually unknown in England as the words "Clanger" and "Fluff" were used to describe broadcasting miscues. At the close of the interview, he said, "Kermit, thanks for your visit and good luck with your Bloomers!!"

Another Blooper of which I was the victim occurred in England. My publisher, Sphere Books, sent me on a promotional tour of various cities in Britain, one of which was Southampton. I was interviewed by Chris Peacock, a young TV personality. We were discussing spoonerisms, the unintended interchange of syllables which is attributed to the Reverend Spooner, the warden of Oxford College, who had the faculty of twisting words. One of the classics uttered by him was a reference to the "Queer Dean," instead of the "Dear Queen." At the end of the program, Chris closed with what had been adlibbed by many TV personalities in the States, such as Johnny Carson and Merv Griffin, "Thank you, Shermit Kafer." Trying to be glib, I snapped back with, "Thank you, Piss Creacock, I mean Piss Peacock . . . thank you very much."

Even Crown Publishers, who publish my books, became a Blooper victim when their printer accidentally put a religious Bible Dictionary between the covers of BEST OF BLOOPERS. What made matters worse was that the Bloopers books were bound into the covers of the Bible Dictionary. You can imagine the confusion and consternation of the recipients of both books.

BLOOPER VICTIMS THE INSIDE STORY

Veteran Newsman Lowell Thomas whose classic on-the-air break ups are preserved for all time by Schafer.

Veteran broadcaster Lowell Thomas will go down in broadcasting history as one of the best-known commentators who has the distinction of being heard by more people throughout the world than any individual. His faculty of "breaking up" and his infectious laughter on the air when something strikes him funny have become legendary. Here is a classic example:

THOMAS: ... about a new book called DIET OR DIE. Author Celeste Geyer, perhaps better known to millions of carnival fans as the one-time Dolly Dimples. Remember, the world's most beautiful fat lady when she weighed 555 pounds, now a svelt 122. She tells in her book how she did it following the advise of a doctor who told her after a near fart ... fartal heart attack to diet or die. (BREAKING UP) The secret to effective weight loss is massive will power, says Mrs. Geyer. (MORE BREAK UP) Well, anyhow, she said her fat friends from carnival life died at an early age and were later buried from the back of a truck. Because they were too big for a hearse. (COMPLETELY DESTROYED).

Talk show hosts, particularly during late night hours, take more liberties than they normally do, knowing some of their shock material can be edited out. Happily, I often get the "outtakes." A classic example of one such shocker, which was not edited, dealt with a Zsa Zsa Gabor guest appearance on Johnny Carson's TONIGHT SHOW. Zsa Zsa sat with a cat on her lap and asked Johnny if he would like to pet her pussy. He reportedly replied, "Sure, if you'd move that damn cat out of the way!!"

The legendary Zsa Zsa Gabor and columnist-writer Sheila Graham.

TV BLOOPER NIGHTMARE OUT OF THE BLUE MOVIE

★ EXTRA ★

THE DAILY Herald

HARD CORE STAG MOVIES SHOCK TV AUDIENCE!!

There is hardly a TV watcher who hasn't conjured up in his or her mind the wild possibility of being witness to the sex act being performed on television ... by accident or by design ... Well, the impossible dream actually happened!!! OUT OF THE BLUE! is a provocative film that documents and preserves all of the shock and hilarity of this unbelievable, but true, incident which startled TV viewers as they were turning in for the night. It was the result of a station employee who screened X-rated films at the TV studio believing the transmitter was off the air! This incredible "Blooper nightmare" has become the TV counterpart of the classic Orson Welles "Invasion from Mars" Halloween eve hoax that petrified radio listeners in 1938. OUT OF THE BLUE! is based on taped phone calls and video tapes which are used in program monitoring for station reference ... Typical phone calls are heard from viewers during the

"action" films ... some callers are outraged ... some loving every minute of it. The documentary was produced by Kermit Schafer in association with Grove Press which pioneered I AM CURIOUS YELLOW in motion picture theatres and was the first to bring adult movies on CATV Television. The film is being shown at colleges throughout the nation.

The following are excerpts from the taped phone calls to the TV station from viewers.

1st CALLER: (OLD LADY) What is the name of this movie that you are showing? I can't find it in my TV GUIDE.

2nd CALLER: (BLACK WOMAN) This movie is far out! The one that I really like is the one with the black socks. He reminds me of someone I used to know.

3rd CALLER: (OWNER OF A BAR) I want to complain about them movies you're showing on TV. It's past closing time, and my customers won't leave the joint.

4th CALLER: (HIGH SCHOOL STUDENT) Wow, these movies are out of sight. I think that it's great that you show sex education on TV.

5th CALLER: (IRATE WOMAN) What kind of movies do you think you're showing on TV? You're supposed to show the Star Spangled Banner and then turn it off.

6th CALLER: (BROOKLYNESE ACCENT) Would you mind telling me who does the casting for these movies? I'd like to try out for a part.

7th CALLER: (SEXY VOICE) These movies are something else. So much more stimulating than watching Johnny Carson and some of those boring late night talk shows.

8th CALLER: This is Father Flanagan. What in the name of the Good Lord is going on at your TV station? Is this a new way to present SERMONETTE? May God have mercy on your soul.

2 GENERATIONS OF EROTICA

Linda Lovelace of DEEP THROAT fame who is the best-known leading lady of adult movies.

Burlesque super star Gypsy Rose Lee who participated in Schafer's record album of Burlesque nostalgia.

THE BLOOPER MOVIE

I have had the good fortune to pioneer many "firsts" in my career in the entertainment world. One such innovation is the first feature-length motion picture featuring my collection of visual Radio and Television Bloopers. This turned out to be a major challenge for me which was made more difficult by some of the less imaginative people in the business of rating films. It is obvious from the remarkable "track record" and from the glowing testimonials from followers from all walks of life, that Bloopers have been accepted in the homes of countless millions in record album and book form. When I transferred this material to the large screen, I was shocked to learn that the same basic material was given an "R" rating. This rating is a sad commentary on how the ratings can be deceptive and misleading as evidence this review in the DETROIT EVENING NEWS, which has the largest circulation of any American evening newspaper.

6-D—THE DETROIT NEWS—Friday, Oct. 4, 1974

Pardon their 'R'

This rating is a blooper!

By A.L. McCLAIN News Entertainment Writer

The silly people who give us our movie ratings are going to guard young ears against hearing those naughty words they listen to every day on the school playground.

"Pardon My Blooper," Kermit Schafer's movie version of his albums and books on the slipups in the broadcasting industry, comes to the screen R-rated.

Meanwhile, films showing gore and violence and brutality are given PG ratings. "The Apprenticeship of Duddy Kravitz" and "Uptown Saturday Night" are two examples playing area theaters.

"BLOOPER" IS a harmless montage of human frailities that occur when people attempt to speak the King's English. It's always hilarious and never offensive. The film doesn't become crude as it seeks out

humor based on the slip of the tongue.

Schafer has spliced together film clips of old television shows that were made in that wonderful era when shows came to us live. With most shows being taped today, the bloopers are erased and lost forever.

THE QUALITY of some of the old clips is bad, but the humor so sharp and clear that audiences aren't likely to complain.

FUNNIEST snafu in the entire film may be the marriage ceremony in which the bride answers "yes" to the question "will you take this woman?"

Schafer has brought some needed laughter into our lives and he has done it without rubbing the skin off his victims.

Take the kids—it certainly won't harm them.

Schafer signs contract with K-tel International for the release of his movie. K-tel also distributes Blooper albums. Shown is Philip Kives, Board Chairman, and Ray Kives, V.P., of the worldwide conglomerate.

At the PARDON MY BLOOPER movie opening at the United Artists theatre in the Westwood suburb of Los Angeles.

MR. BLOOPER VISITS CAMPUSES

Bloopers are now an attraction on the college and lecture circuit where Schafer presents a one-man, multi-media, 2-hour show entitled The BLUNDERFUL WORLD OF BLOOPERS. Audio and video tape, together with film, are packaged into a program of entertainment. Shown is an appearance at Shriver Hall at Johns Hopkins University in Baltimore, Maryland. Also shown are promotional appearances.

NEWSPAPER—BALTIMORE SUN

RADIO—WBAL BALTIMORE

TV—WMAR-TV BALTIMORE

JOHNS HOPKINS UNIVERSITY, BALTIMORE

Stage and screen actress Barbara Rush appearing on Baltimore TV talk show with Schafer.

BLOOPERS IN EDUCATION LINGUISTIC ANALYSIS

David Frost who devoted an entire program to linguistic analysis on which Bloopers played a prominent role. Frost is relating a spoonerism he committed in a dramatic show on which he had the line "Truss the victim up with a tie." However, he blooped, "Tie the victim up with a truss!"

Included in the David Frost TV Special were Stuart B. Flexner, Senior Editor of the New Edition of the RANDOM HOUSE DICTIONARY, and opera and stage star Dorothy Sarnoff who has become interested in speech analysis. She authored a book SPEECH CAN CHANGE YOUR LIFE.

Blooperology is a subject that is used in the academic field at all educational levels. In an article on "Phonemic and Analogic Lapses in Radio and Television Speech" for the scholarly journal AMERICAN SPEECH, published by the Columbia University Press, R. C. Simonini, Jr., Chairman of the Department of English at a Virginia university wrote, "Blooper records are a rich source of contemporary material for linguistic analysis." Shown below is another application of Bloopers in education.

Teacher's Edition   <u>THINK-AND-DO BOOK</u>   Scott, Foresman and Company

Performers on radio and TV programs sometimes make funny mistakes by mixing up their words. Read the sentences and draw a line under the words that are mixed up. Then write the words the person meant to say on the dotted line.

On a TV cooking program, the cook said, "Here's a new way to prepare picken chie."

A radio announcer rushed in and said, "I was held up by the drain and rizzle."

Presenting the homemaker of the week, the radio announcer said, "Here is our homely friendmaker."

A news reporter talking about a visiting king and queen said, "When they arrive, you will hear a twenty-one sun galute."

During an advertisement one announcer said, "When you use this poison, all mats and rice will disappear."

"The forecast for today is shattered scowers," said the weather reporter.

A woman showing how to set a table said, "Put the sporks and foons here."

A sports reporter said of the man who lost the fight, "He looked as though he received a blushing crow."

On a program about farm animals, the announcer said, "Here come the chucks and dickens."

As he spoke of the history of a foreign country, the TV teacher said, "Then the kingquering congs took over."

BLOOPERS IN PRINT NEWSPAPERS / MAGAZINES / BOOKS

Johnny Carson said, "Bloopers read about as funny as when they occur on the air," as evidence several Crown best-seller Blooper books and the half dozen Fawcett World Library paperbacks. Bloopers have been sought after by national publications for regular features with diverse readership, such as READER'S DIGEST and PLAYBOY Magazine. Also at opposite ends of the spectrum have been regular features in WOMAN'S DAY and NATIONAL ENQUIRER, in which Schafer started the long-running weekly "Spot the Blooper" Contest. COSMOPOLITAN, CORONET, and McCALL's readers have also been treated to Bloopers as a regular feature.

Reader's Digest

Slip of the Lip

𝓕ROM *Blunderful World of Bloopers,* Kermit Schafer's collection of broadcasting boners:

"THE SIX A.M. forecast is for partly croudy with a 75-percent chance of rain mixed with sleep early this morning."

AN ANNOUNCER blooped: "Another delicious combination for these hot days is a chilled grease sandwich and a choke."

"WE WILL CONTINUE with our program of uninterrupted music after this message from our sponsor."

"FOR EXCITEMENT and beautiful girls, see color cleverage of the Rose Bowl Game, New Year's Day on CBS."

"AFTER A FAST INCREASE this morning, Wall Street storks dropped nine pints on the Dow-Jones averages."

"ALSO KEEPING AN EYE on the Woodstock Rock Festival was New York's Governor Rockin Nelsenfeller."

AT THE LAUNCHING of a ship in Norway, a local announcer declared: "The Duchess handled it beautifully, smashing the champagne bottle against the prow with the aplomb of an expert. The crowd cheered as she majestically slid down the runway into the sea." —Published by Crown

202

DIAL-A-BLOOPER HOW IT WORKS

In the continuing challenges for innovative applications of Bloopers in varied media, Schafer has brought the humor of Bloopers to millions of telephone subscribers by special arrangement with the New York Telephone Company. Dial-A-Blooper is brought into the homes of listeners by way of the phone company's Dial-A-Joke series. Each caller hears one minute of Bloopers, for which a charge is added to his phone bill, which is played on a continuous cassette. Blooper segments are changed every day. Below is a sample.

DIAL-A-BLOOPER

SCHAFER: Hello, this is Kermit Schafer with excerpts from my collection of Radio and TV Bloopers.

ANNOUNCER: That is why we are the largest producer in the United States of magnoosium, aleeminum, and stool.

CONTESTANT: I work for the Pittsburgh Natural Gas Company. Over 90 percent of the people in Pittsburgh have gas.

NEWSCASTER: Scotch Soup covers the nose ... NEWS!

ANNOUNCER: "Evening Melodies" is heard one hour earlier if your community is on Eastern Standard Time, one hour later if ... well, there is a two-hour difference in certain cities ... Oh, to hell with it!

ANNOUNCER: Ladies, do you wake up in the morning feeling lustless ... er, listless?

COMMENTATOR: All the world was thrilled with the marriage of the Duck and Doochess of Windsor.

ANNOUNCER: And now it is time for your Homely Friend Maker ... I mean Friendly Home Maker!

EMCEE: Ladies and Gentlemen, the great banjoist Eddie Playbody will now pee for you ... EDDIE PEABODY!

NEWSCASTER: Our neighbors over in Columbia, Tennessee, the largest outdoor mule market in the world, held a Jackass Parade headed by the Governor.

ANNOUNCER: And Dad will love the delicious flavor too ... So, remember, it's Wonder Bread for the breast in bed!

SCHAFER: Thank you for calling. Call again soon for another DIAL-A-BLOOPER.

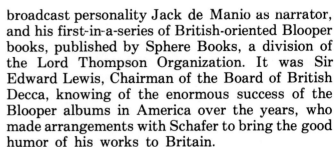

BUNGLES FOR BRITAIN

The phone rang and was answered by April Kelly, Schafer's efficient, all-around girl Friday. "It's London calling . . . Bob Holness from BBC Radio . . . He has David Hamilton standing by for a live interview on his 'Late Night Extra' program." In seconds Schafer was on the air live in London relating the latest news from Bloopersville. In a reply to a request for the latest Nixon Blooper, Schafer related the one about the news announcer who said, "The rumor that the President would veto the bill came from high White Horse souses." He could hear the chuckling through the telephone receiver followed by a "Jolly good!"

Schafer is now a part-time London resident, as a result of the acclaim which has come to him from abroad for his brilliant capture of broadcasting's unintended indiscretions before microphone and camera. He is described in a feature article in the LONDON DAILY EXPRESS as a "fluff buff". In Britain, the equivalent of "Blooper" is fluff, clanger or boob. Schafer introduced the word "Blooper" in England, a word he is credited with having coined.

Schafer recently appeared on a dozen radio and TV programs in England, in connection with a promotional tour which took him from London to Bristol, Birmingham, Southampton, Wales, and other British provinces. On this extensive tour, he introduced the first-of-a-series of hilarious British versions of PARDON MY BLOOPER, released by British Decca, featuring well-known BBC broadcast personality Jack de Manio as narrator, and his first-in-a-series of British-oriented Blooper books, published by Sphere Books, a division of the Lord Thompson Organization. It was Sir Edward Lewis, Chairman of the Board of British Decca, knowing of the enormous success of the Blooper albums in America over the years, who made arrangements with Schafer to bring the good humor of his works to Britain.

In London Schafer visited the hallowed studios of BBC's Broadcast House for radio interviews. He also appeared as a guest on some of BBC-TV's top television programs spreading the Blooper gospel. "If there is such a thing as the thrill of a lifetime, it was when the good old sacrosanct BBC played and televised samplings of Bloopers from my collection, including many considered too provocative by American standards. The British appear to have relaxed somewhat in their stuffy feelings about material once considered taboo. For instance, the delightful double-meaning broadcast by an unwitting school teacher during her popular program 'Music and Movements for Infants' several years ago, which dealt with children dancing with imaginary balls. The BBC had become super sensitive about the incident when they learned underground recordings of it were being made and were distributed illicitly. They reportedly would fire any of their personnel caught with or listening to this memorable broadcast, which is now a prized collector's item."

UPI recently carried a feature which papers printed under the headline "THE BLOOPER SCOOPER TAKES ON BBC." The story contained the first annual list of the Ten Best British Bloopers. A loyal army of new British Blooper fans has been adding to next year's nominations, with contributions such as the one from Richard Whiteley, a Yorkshire television presenter of the program CALENDAR, "Every commentator dreads State occasions featuring the Royal Horse Artillery. More than one has described them as the Queen's Troop, the Royal Arse Hortillery."

Today's attitude regarding this unique type of humor is perhaps best summed up in the words of BBC's Jack de Manio, who, in his introduction to Schafer's first Blooper book in England, says, "I do believe that Kermit Schafer has rendered a service to the broadcasting industry by relaxing the enormous strains and tensions of those of us who are involved in it."

As one who has a great admiration for the British people, Schafer had always hoped some day to share the humor of his works with them. The time has finally arrived.

The Blooper albums are enshrined in the BBC Gramophone Library located in Broadcast House, London, England.

Sir Edward Lewis, Chairman of the Board of British Decca record company, brings Bloopers to Britain.

Kermit Schafer autographs his new Blooper book for the producer of Pebble Mill TV program, originating from Birmingham, England, after appearing on the popular BBC-TV network show.

Schafer is greeted by Sphere Book Publishers' representative in Southampton, England, on one of the multi – British province promotional tour stopovers.

Radio Luxemburg interviews Schafer at the British Decca press reception given in his honor. Also shown is Virginia Hadley, who interviewed him for a feature article which appeared in the LONDON DAILY EXPRESS.

BBC broadcast personality, Jack de Manio, who narrates the British-oriented PARDON MY BLOOPER record albums for Decca, at Sphere Books' press reception given Schafer.

Producer Schafer is interviewed on the Lord Harlech TV station in Bristol, England.

VIDEOTAPE ARCHIVES

BLOOPERS PRESERVED

Museum of Broadcasting

Located only a block from CBS TV headquarters in midtown Manhattan, the Museum of Broadcasting opened in 1976 with a collection of 350 radio and television programs. Back in 1967, William Paley, Chairman of CBS, commissioned a study of existing broadcast archives, and the need for a major institution to preserve broadcast materials became apparent. Paley then undertook the development and funding of what he has described as "a public resource for enjoyment and information relating to broadcasting."

The Museum's president is Robert Saudek, who produced "Omnibus" and several other TV shows. More than 1,500 television programs have been catalogued in the collection so far, many of them dating back to the 1950's. With the Chairmen of NBC, ABC, CBS, and the Corporation for Public Broadcasting as members of its Board of Trustees, the Museum has free access to network video tapes. In fact, each network guarantees the Museum a certain number of programs every month. The curator selects shows on the basic of intrinsic value, awards won, high Nielsen ratings, and landmark value (such as the debut of Judy Garland or the first use of split-screen technology).

William Paley tries out a video carrel at the Museum of Broadcasting (right) as Robert Saudek, the Museum's president, looks on. CBS funded the Museum.

Schafer arriving at the Museum of Broadcasting in New York City which preserves his Blooper works.

Robert Saudek, Museum President, greets Schafer.

"Mr. Blooper" enjoying his BLUNDERFUL WORLD OF BLOOPERS donation to the Museum. The collection will be housed in its own Blooper Hall of Fame.

B.P.I. YEAR BOOK 1976
THE BRITISH PHONOGRAPHIC INDUSTRY

WORLD'S BIGGEST SELLING ALBUMS

YEAR OF ORIGINAL RELEASE	TITLE	ARTIST	CURRENT RIGHTS U.K. LABEL	ESTIMATED WORLD SALES (MILLIONS)
1965	THE SOUND OF MUSIC	SOUNDTRACK	RCA	14 +
1958	LITTLE DRUMMER BOY*	HARRY SIMEONE CHORALE BEATLES	20th CENTURY	13 +
1958	SOUTH PACIFIC	SOUNDTRACK	RCA	8 +
1967	SERGEANT PEPPER'S LONELY HEARTS CLUB BAND	BEATLES	APPLE	7
1970	BRIDGE OVER TROUBLED WATER	SIMON AND GARFUNKEL	CBS	6 +
1968	THE BEATLES – DOUBLE LP	BEATLES	CBS	6 +
1956	MY FAIR LADY	ORIGINAL CAST	CBS	6 +
1964	MARY POPPINS	SOUNDTRACK		6
1961	WEST SIDE STORY	SOUNDTRACK	CBS	6
1963	MEET THE BEATLES †	BEATLES	APPLE	6
1962	THE FIRST FAMILY	VAUGHN MEADER	CBS	5½ +
1968	HAIR	ORIGINAL CAST	RCA	5 +
1965	WIPPED CREAM AND OTHER DELIGHTS	HERB ALPERT and the TIJUANA BRASS	A and M	5 +
1969	ABBEY ROAD	BEATLES	APPLE	5 +
1966	THE MONKEES	MONKEES	BELL	5
1967	MORE OF THE MONKEES	MONKEES	BELL	5
1953	RADIO BLOOPERS	KERMIT SCHAEFFER	⊕	4¾ +
1963	JOHN FITZGERALD KENNEDY	A MEMORIAL ALBUM	■	4 +
1963	RUBBER SOUL	BEATLES	APPLE	3½ +
1959	KNOCKERS UP	RUSTY WARREN	⊕	3½ +
1970	LET IT BE	BEATLES	APPLE	3½
1970	HEY JUDE	BEATLES	APPLE	3½
1964	BEATLES '65‡	BEATLES	APPLE	3½
1967	MAGICAL MYSTERY TOUR	BEATLES	APPLE	3 +
1969	LED ZEPPELIN 2	LED ZEPPELIN	ATLANTIC	3 +
1968	IN-A-GADDA-DA-VIDA	IRON BUTTERFLY	ATLANTIC	3
1949§	OKLAHHOMA	ORIGINAL CAST	MCA	3
1949	SOUTH PACIFIC	ORIGINAL CAST	CBS	3
1961	BLUE HAWAII	ELVIS PRESLEY	RCA	3
1964	A HARD DAY'S NIGHT	BEATLES	APPLE	2½ +
1966	S.R.O	HERB ALBERT and the TIJUANA BRASS	A and M	2½ +
1958	TSCHAIKOUSKY PIANO CONCERTO No.1	VAN CLIBURN	RCA	2½ +
1964	GOLDFINGER	SOUNDTRACK	UNITED ARTISTS	2¼ +
1960	THE SOUND OF MUSIC	ORIGINAL CAST	CBS	2½
1957	WEST SIDE STORY	ORIGINAL CAST	CBS	2½
1965	GOING PLACES	HERB ALPERT and the TIJUANA BRASS	A and M	2 +
1966	WHAT NOW MY LOVE?	HERB ALPERT and the TIJUANA BRASS	A and M	2 +
1966	REVOLVER	BEATLES	APPLE	2 +
1966	BALLADS OF THE GREEN BERETS	S/SGT BARRY SADLER	RCA	2 +
1965	LOOK AT US	SONNY AND CHER	ATLANTIC	2 +
1962	MOON RIVER	ANDY WILLIAMS	CBS	2 +
1962	MODERN SOUNDS IN COUNTRY AND WESTERN MUSIC	RAY CHARLES	ABC	2 +
1958	JOHNNY'S GREATEST HITS	JOHNNY MATHIS	CBS	2 +
1962	PETER, PAUL AND MARY	PETER, PAUL and MARY	WARNER	2 +
1966	DOCTOR ZHIVAGO	SOUNDTRACK	MGM	2 +
1967	HEADQUARTERS	MONKEES	BELL	2 +
1966	BIG HITS – HIGH TIDE AND GREEN GRASS	ROLLING STONES	DECCA	2 +
1956	HYMNS	TENNESSEE ERNIE FORD	CAPITOL	2 +
1967	BLOOMING HITS	PAUL MAURIAT and his ORCHESTRA	PHILIPS	2 +
1970	JOHN LENNON/PLASTIC ONO BAND	JOHN LENNON/PLASTIC ONO BAND	APPLE	2 +
1970	ALL THINGS MUST PASS	GEORGE HARRISON	APPLE	2 +
1970	LED ZEPPELIN III	LED ZEPPELIN	ATLANTIC	2 +
1970	DEJA VU	CROSBY, STILLS, NASH AND YOUNG	ATLANTIC	2 +

×   Originally titled 'Sing we now of Christmas' — British release titled 'Salute to Christmas.
†   Issued in U.K. as 'With the Beatles
‡   Issued in U.K. as 'Beatles for Sale
§   Originally issued in 1943 on 78 r.p.m. Achieved main sales following 33⅓ r.p.m. released in 1949.
⊕   No U.K. outlet for American Jubilee label.
■   No U.K. outlet for American Premier label.
Including only records issued prior to 1971 and sales figures for those years prior to 1972.

242

PART4: INDEX

ABOUT THE AUTHOR AND BLOOPER HISTORY

BLOOPER CATEGORIES

GENERAL INDEX